I would not call

conversational, a

shrewd in seeing th ...ions of the gospel. He brings to expression the local radicality of the gospel as concerns missional urgency. Readers will be drawn to a fresh understanding of the gospel for a society that does not value our bodily existence very much. The word *dangerous* is exactly right for what Butler has in mind.

—WALTER BRUEGGEMANN, Columbia Theological Seminary

There is much talk about the deterioration of cities today both in the religious and secular worlds. Many folks are trying to figure it out from a distance. Jason has plunged into the city finding Christ's presence there. Reading these pages you will be compelled to go on a risky walk with God. Your view of the city will be radically transformed. This is not a "how-to" book; this is a call to brokenness.

—JO ANNE LYON, General Superintendent, The Wesleyan Church

At International Justice Mission, I have the privilege of working with a diverse group of churches and pastors united by their passion for answering God's call to seek justice. Jason Butler is one of these friends, and in *Dangerous Presence* it becomes clear why his pursuit of justice in the city and the world has born so much fruit: because he is willing to do what is uncomfortable and difficult and be shaped by God in the process. May his passion and openness to God's call encourage you as you read his powerful story.

—JIM MARTIN, vice president of church mobilization at International Justice Mission, author of *The Just Church*

Jason Butler chooses transparency and courage as his way of not only bringing life to the city of Milwaukee, but also challenging the rest of us to move outside the boundaries of self-pursuit. His character, confidence, and tenacity are both challenging and humbling. In *Dangerous Presence*, he will challenge your definition of *pastor* and take you beyond the edges of whatever you think leadership is or is not. If you have the courage to take in some straight talk and allow God to reshape your definition of *ministry*, then this book is a must-read for you. Jason is the kind of leader the church has been waiting for.

—HEATHER SEMPLE, lead pastor,
Red Cedar Community Church, Rice Lake, Wisconsin

The cocoon in which we have insulated ourselves from the pain in our cities is suffocating us. In *Dangerous Presence*, Jason Butler has issued an invitation for us to claw our way out of the insulation and connect our destiny to the destiny of urban America in order to breathe the air of the kingdom of God. It is a call to reorient our vision of ourselves, God, and his kingdom by changing our location. Writing in an engaging, folksy style full of personality, Jason draws us into his story and the story of his friends in Milwaukee, Wisconsin. It is a story that woos us into drawing near to our brothers and sisters who live in urban poverty. *Dangerous Presence* is a song of lament and praise, and once it gets stuck in your head, it will be hard to forget.

—SCOTT BESSENECKER, associate director of missions,
InterVarsity Christian Fellowship, Madison, Wisconsin

DANGEROUS PRESENCE

FOLLOWING JESUS INTO THE CITY

JASON BUTLER

wesleyan
publishing
house

Indianapolis, Indiana

Published by Wesleyan Publishing House
Indianapolis, Indiana 46250
Printed in the United States of America
ISBN: 978-0-89827-751-7
ISBN (e-book): 978-0-89827-752-4

Library of Congress Cataloging-in-Publication Data

Butler, Jason, 1979-
Dangerous presence : following Jesus into the city / Jason Butler.
pages cm
Includes bibliographical references.
ISBN 978-0-89827-751-7 (pbk.) -- ISBN 978-0-89827-752-4 1. City missions. 2. Cities and towns--Religious aspects--Christianity. 3. Risk taking (Psychology)--Religious aspects--Christianity. 4. Distributive justice--Religious aspects--Christianity. I. Title.
BV2653.B88 2013
253.09173'2--dc23

2013027968

This book is dedicated to the members and staff of Transformation City Church.

I am continually amazed and in awe of how you follow Jesus into hard places, of how you seek justice and mercy and grace and peace. You show me what it looks like for a community of faith to live for something bigger than yourselves. Thank you.

CONTENTS

FOREWORD

This book reminds me of the words from John as written in *The Message*: "The Word became flesh . . . and moved into the neighborhood" (John 1:14). Truly this is what has happened. Jason not only discusses incarnational ministry theoretically, but leads us on the journey of the reality. I have had the privilege of sharing this journey with Jason over the past five years through regular communication. Each time we talked, I was amazed at how God was opening doors. But on the other side, I realized that with each open door Jason was becoming a "learner," which meant it was making him more vulnerable and humble. He did not start this with grandiose ideas of his own strength, but of his own weakness. Sometimes the learning even made him feel weaker. But in reading this book, I believe through Jason's honesty the reader will understand more deeply another text written in the crucible of pain by Paul: "But he said to me, 'My grace is sufficient for you, for my power is made perfect in weakness'" (2 Cor. 12:9).

When I first toured the dirty, smelly, dingy archery center that Jason and the congregation had found to possibly redo for their church, I thought, "This is going to take more than just a remodel; this is going to need some type of radical transformation." The next time I was there, I thought I was walking into another building. Transformation to the building had truly happened. But more, there was the "dangerous presence" of Christ in the people from all walks of life humming through the building. It was electric!

Walking through the neighborhood with Jason and his staff recently, I had the same experience: people calling from their porches greetings of joy, love, and acceptance. Trust continues to build. But the dangerous presence is more than about living in a different neighborhood or culture. What is found on these pages is about personal and cultural transformation through the power of the Holy Spirit. This is not about a "do gooder" project for a selected period of time. This is about a lifetime of living. This is about a call of biblical mandate. This is about the Jesus life.

Jason leads us through biblical examples that shake one's comfort zone. It is my prayer that through reading this we will have an army of people who declare, "I want to join the risk of being a dangerous presence with Jesus wherever that may lead." I am joining that declaration!

—JO ANNE LYON
General Superintendent, The Wesleyan Church

INTRODUCTION

Risk cannot be taught. Some people seem wired to naturally seek out risk; others have a great aversion to it. A person's willingness to risk comes from a passion deep within the soul. Risk is when we willingly make a sacrifice for the possibility of bringing good to ourselves, others, or the world.

This is not a "how to" book. You will not learn the ten steps to urban ministry in these pages. Instead, this book is about the division and barriers that exist between our society and the American city. It is a critique of our culture's deep, underlying values that separate us from one another and bring a paralyzing fear into our lives, minds, and ministries.

Please understand that I am writing to inspire people to engage in urban ministry. Are all people called to urban ministry? No. Do I think all people are called to relocate to serve in a city? No. But I do believe that every follower of Jesus is called to serve the poor, fight injustice, and bring compassion to our world. Because of this, I believe we all have to consider the call to the city or an urban center, because it is in our urban centers that we see the highest concentration of the poor and marginalized in our society.

It is my deep belief that God is calling the church to the broken urban centers of our nation and world. This book is my attempt—through the stories, accounts, and teachings that have been a valuable part of my journey as a pastor leading an urban church—to inspire you to follow Jesus into the under-resourced neighborhoods in our nation and your own backyard. To follow Jesus to do one distinct thing: love.

This is fundamentally a book about love—about God's love for us and for the urban oppressed and marginalized. It is about how these two loves find their union within urban ministry.

Following Jesus as he announces this love is risky, but then again, following Jesus is always risky. Risk, by definition, means that the journey is not guaranteed to turn out the way you envision or desire it to turn out. Risk always comes with a cloud of uncertainty.

My hope is that this book will help you to take a deep look at the culture in which you are immersed and how that culture can hijack your God-given imagination so that engaging in urban ministry seems too scary, too impossible, and too difficult.

This story of fear and anxiety is a false story. But Jesus has another story for you to live in. A story of grace. A story of hope. A story of love.

As you read, may you be inspired in a new way to stand up and follow Jesus as he journeys into the city. May you learn to love and not fear. May you bring unity and not division. And may you put on the cloak of obedience as you take off the tattered rags of worldly ambition.

As you do this, may you become a restorer of broken-down walls. May you turn over the tables of injustice and oppression. May you become a dangerous presence.

1

ORANGE PEELS

I remember the first time I saw a kid eating an orange peel. It was one of those moments where time stands still—all at once it seems giant boulders have fallen from heaven upon the delicate tapestry of hope.

As I watched, I felt as if one of these boulders from heaven fell on me. It crushed me. It challenged deeply held beliefs about the world and my place in it. It left my worldview shattered in a thousand different pieces—thrown like shrapnel all around where I was standing.

I lost something that day, something I will never be able to regain. I lost my blindness.

Oh, how I sometimes wish I could regain the bliss of lack of sight, but I can't seem to find it anywhere. Like someone took it—hid it from me in some cruel, divine joke.

This dramatic shift—in my assumptions about the world and my place in it—all happened in the most unlikely of places. I was a missionary intern in an orphan summer camp in a remote Russian village named Lyahi (Lay-hee).

.ı was a hard place to live. It was truly in the middle of ..ere, on the banks of some big Russian river with a name .n't even pronounce. It was a village in every way, one that .eemed to come right out of pre-Soviet Russia. Few homes had running water. Only one store sometimes carried bread and most of the time didn't have any. There were no cars—well, maybe two, at most. There were few ways in and even fewer ways out. The most exciting thing to do in this village was to walk out to the edge of the field and watch the local shepherd bring in the goats and cattle from a day of grazing in the countryside. Seriously.

And in the middle of this village was an orphanage. It was not just any orphanage. The Lyahi Orphanage was where they sent the kids who did not fit in—those with a physical or mental disability, the outcasts, the troublemakers. A little like Misfit Island.

I wasn't ready for what I saw that day. I didn't have time to begin the pre-rehabilitation process. It happened too fast, all at once, like a flash flood in a Los Angeles spillway. I'm just riding my skateboard, then all of a sudden, a wall of water sweeps me away.

I hadn't come to Russia for this anyway. I was there because at the moment I didn't have anything better to do with my life. It was my second trip to Russia. On the first, I had met a girl, and, well, if you meet a girl on your first trip, then you will usually take a second trip.

I was twenty-two, had just finished college, and was in love. I thought I could do a little good by hanging with some orphans in a summer camp. I could pursue the girl while "preaching the gospel" to these kids. I felt pretty good about myself . . . up until the moment I was crushed.

I was doing the missionary thing, saving lost souls of orphan children. I collected great stories to put in a newsletter to send back home.

I was living the high life. I was well on my way to a promising Christian career. I was on the fast track. People said things like, "You have such a promising life of serving Jesus in front of you." If I were a balloon, I would have floated away from all the helium people were filling me with.

And then it happened.

One afternoon after I had finished my orphanage cafeteria lunch—a small portion of river fish and buckwheat (I lost some serious weight that summer, and I was already a pretty small guy)—I was hanging out with the kids before our afternoon program. I saw a group of kids under a tree with oranges they had been given by the missionary team. They ate their oranges like a hungry pack of wolves.

At first it didn't surprise me. I was pretty hungry too. But then they did something I had never seen before. They took the peels—the remnants of their post-lunch treat—and instead of throwing them away, ate them. The kids were eating the orange peels.

Remember that boulder from heaven? This is when it hit me.

Maybe you thought it would be something more shocking or dramatic. Maybe you're thinking, "You mean orange peels changed your life?"

Yes, they did. Well, not exactly the orange peels—the boulder did. The orange peels just tripped the device that cut the wire holding the massive rock over my head. What a sinister cosmic trap.

Who can say what such a moment will be for you or anyone else? For me, it was seeing kids eating orange peels. And it was me trying to reconcile what I had just witnessed to the life I had been living.

As the boulder rolled off of my soul, I was left with a lot of questions. I remember thinking, "Why in the world are those kids eating orange peels? Do they actually like them?" I actually asked someone that question. And I still remember the answer: "They were eating orange peels because they didn't know when they would get their next meal."

When you see children eating orange peels, it leaves wounds—wounds that might not ever heal properly because they have questions attached to them: How can we live in a world where kids in Lyahi eat orange peels and Americans spend twenty billion dollars a year on ice cream?[1] How did I just spend eighty-five thousand dollars on a four-year private liberal arts college education and another fifteen hundred dollars on a plane ticket to Russia to "share the gospel," and this kid right in front of me is starving and doesn't know where his next meal will come from?

Kids eating orange peels is injustice. It's not the way the world should be. It shows something is wrong, and we realize it the moment we see it. It's like a flash bang of brokenness that momentarily paralyzes our senses.

Or maybe that was the rock.

Seeing this paralyzed me. Left me grieving. Angry. In despair. It left me wondering, "What can I do about this?" I could give money, but would that money actually get to the kids? Hard to say. I could buy more oranges or food, but how long would it last? Not long enough.

The answer to my question left me even more unsettled. The one thing I could do that might actually benefit the children was to live there. Move to Lyahi. Take up residence. Change my proximity. Call this place home. Move to the neighborhood. Be part of their lives on a long-term basis, where my proximity was not far but rather close. To be part of their suffering.

The kids didn't really need my money; they needed my life. But to give them that, I would have to live with them.

Life's toughest questions are usually answered by proximity. To make a difference, I would have to change my proximity to the problem—get closer, more personal.

The answers to injustice aren't first found in government funding or United Nations programs. Answers start with one person getting hit with a heavenly boulder and then making a choice to get close to the problem.

Injustice begins to break down when someone chooses to move closer.

That's the whole premise of this book. That's my "aha" statement. In case you missed it let me say it again: Injustice begins to break down when someone chooses to move closer.

On the flipside, injustices are magnified when we choose to look the other direction, to move farther away.

But that's what we tend to do, isn't it? When the plague breaks out, we get out of town for our own safety. When there is a war, we flee the country back to the safety of American soil. When crime overtakes our cities, we move to the suburbs or to the country to get some "peace and quiet." To ease the pain of our souls, we move away, because moving closer demands too much. To move close, we have to make sacrifices.

Moving closer to injustice is risky. It's dangerous. It may cost us more than we are prepared to give. Getting close enough to feel the breath of injustice or hear its victims screaming in the night is scary. Moving into a neighborhood where the pimp of injustice is in charge is not the automatic choice many of us will make.

Lyahi was not just a remote village in Russia. It was designed to be a ghetto. A nice country ghetto where goats and cows come in from their long days of grazing, but a ghetto nonetheless. The village was in the middle of nowhere—hard to get to, hard to get out of. Buses didn't go there very often, and only a small number of people had cars. It was the perfect location for the government to send the kids they didn't want in their cities—the "troubled" kids, the kids with mental disorders or learning disorders, or just downright trouble makers.

Lyahi was like the Russian orphanage version of colonial Australia—a penal colony for the worst of the worst. We ship the kids there, and then we don't have to see them again or deal with them roaming the streets of our cities or towns. Ship them to Lyahi where there is no way out. This was the way they wanted it.

Ghettos don't just happen. They are planned and sustained by people who don't want the people inside to get out.

Think that's offensive? Well, it is. Think I'm wrong? Then try to get out of one.

A *ghetto*, as I will use the term, is not based on race or culture, but rather a place where people live in inescapable poverty, oppression, or injustice. Ghettos can be in rural villages like Lyahi, urban centers like Chicago, in the prairies of the West called "reservations," or even in the suburbs where people are suffering because they are disconnected from everyone. Ghettos can be physical or spiritual. Ghettos are all around us, and you may even be living in one today without realizing it.

The organization I worked with tries to get some of the kids out. Here and there a few kids are adopted and begin new lives. This is good, but hard. It costs many thousands of dollars to get one kid out. And then there's no guarantee that the adoption will go well. Many of the kids are so broken from years in the orphanage that they simply cannot adjust to life in the West.

The only way to make a difference in the lives of these children is to change one's proximity. No, let me rephrase that statement. The only way for *me* to make a difference in the lives of these children was to change *my* proximity. To intentionally relocate. To go and live in this village of Lyahi. To live close and be a constant presence in their lives. To build, buy, or rent a place to live, and go live there—long term—with these kids. To feel their pain each day. To truly know what life is like in this village. To gain their trust and be part of their daily lives for years to come.

That would be love.

But I didn't love them. I loved me more. I didn't move there. None of us did. Of the hundred or so missionaries who came and went from Lyahi, none of us moved there. All of us left with broken hearts at the pain of the children's circumstances, but none of us did what we needed to do.

Moving to this small ghetto would have been hard and would have cost much. Indeed, it would have cost our whole lives. I was young and had to finish my education. I had to get married and have some kids. I had to have a career for myself in the church world. I wanted to be known, respected. I needed to save some money, start a retirement fund, pay off student loans, buy an engagement ring. There were so many things I had to do. So many things I had to experience. Besides, they didn't even have running water in this village!

Moving to Lyahi would have cost me my career, my future. It was risky. It was dangerous to my future. The cost was too high.

So I came home and left the kids eating their orange peels.

DILUTED JUICE

In our house, we buy organic juice. We buy most things organic and local because we think this is a better and more sustainable way to shop and eat. But it's expensive, and it is sometimes a stretch for us. So we dilute our juice.[2] Jesus could turn water into wine, but we can turn one jar of juice into five or six! Little miracles. We just pour some undiluted, fully potent juice into another jar, add a little Stevia, and fill the rest of the jar with water. (Stevia is a sweet herb that has zero calories and none of the negative side effects of sugar.) It's brilliant, really. It saves lots of money. We've been doing this for a while, and we have gotten so used to it that we don't even like to drink undiluted juice. It's too strong, too potent. We like our diluted stuff more.

I think many of us have diluted the message of Scripture the same way my family dilutes juice. In order to get more people in the doors and to stretch out the "product," we've taken the hard and difficult message of Jesus, the message that will cost us much, and we've diluted it down to a version that is more palatable, sweeter, and will be easier on our budgets.

The Scriptures give us examples of Jesus giving people this real, undiluted version of God's call on their lives. Sometimes people embraced it; sometimes people did not. Sometimes we need to see people who walked away from Jesus to give us a bearing on our direction. Are we like the ones leaving Jesus? Or are we like the ones following Jesus? One of those examples of people being overwhelmed by the difficult words of Jesus comes in Matthew 8:19. A young man came to Jesus and wanted to follow him—lingo for becoming a disciple of Jesus, entering into Jesus' *talmid*, being a "wise student" or pupil of the rabbi.

"Then a teacher of the law came to him and said, 'Teacher, I will follow you wherever you go.' Jesus replied, 'Foxes have dens and birds have nests, but the Son of Man has no place to lay his head.' Another disciple said to him, 'Lord, first let me go and bury my father.' But Jesus told him, 'Follow me, and let the dead bury their own dead'" (Matt. 8:19–22).

This might seem harsh at first—Jesus calling someone to leave his dying father on his deathbed and follow him. Wow, Jesus, can't you be a little more "family friendly"? But this has nothing to do with that. When a father was on his deathbed, the son was required by Jewish Law to sit with him, sitting *shiv'ah*.[3] Nope, this guy wanted to go home and live some more, wait till his father died, collect his inheritance, set up his retirement fund, save for his kids' college tuition, and then, when everything was in order, come back and follow Jesus. This guy wanted to limit his risk. He wanted the benefits of following Jesus without the cost.

Jesus didn't like when people tried to limit their risk. Another famous instance is the narrative of the rich young ruler. A wealthy, young landowner came to Jesus and said, "Good teacher, what must I do to inherit eternal life?" (Luke 18:18). Notice that only wealthy people asked Jesus this question about eternal life. Poor people have so much to deal with in the present moment that their prayers to Jesus are "Save us!" or "Heal us!" or "Feed us!" The poor understand that eternal life, or life in the age to come, starts right now with things being set right in the right now. The wealthy—who would have much to lose if the world were set right in the present—are often more concerned with life in the age to come.

This explains a lot about America's fixation on heaven and its aversion to the biblical idea of "shalom" (peace) in the present.

Being part of a present moment where everything is in harmony, peace, and a healed state usually requires those who have power, wealth, and influence to give it up for those who don't. That's why the rich young ruler asked the question about life later on, in the future, in some faraway place that had nothing to do with right here, right now. And that's why Jesus' response was so challenging to him. Because Jesus knew there needs to be healing now to have healing later. So Jesus looked at the young man with compassion and said, "Sell everything you have and give it to the poor" (Luke 18:22).

Jesus was saying that life in the age to come is linked with life in the present moment. Healing then is linked to healing now. Justice then is linked to justice now. Jesus was saying, "Open your eyes and see the world around you. See that in order to have life in the age to come you need to begin life now. So go and sell all you have and set things right around you. Break down the walls you have built up between you and your poor neighbor. You've been profiting on the backs of the poor for a long time. Stop it. In order to save yourself, let go of your money and power and empower and bless those around you. Then you will see what life is all about. Then you will see heaven crash into earth, and you won't bring me silly questions any longer about how to have life in the age to come, because you will realize that abundant life now will carry over for eternity."

That is a hard answer. It's undiluted juice. The young man walked away, with his wealth intact, sad. He could not give up his present privilege for future peace. So he had neither.

Often we dilute this message of the rich young ruler, don't we? In America we are rich, and this message is hard. Sell all you have. No, Jesus didn't really mean that. It was all just a test, right? If the rich young ruler would have agreed, Jesus would have said, "Psych! Gotcha! You passed the test. All I wanted to see was the pure intention of your heart."

Diluted.

He told some other followers that to follow him they would have to "take up their cross and follow" him (Mark 8:34). Today we reinterpret this statement to mean that we have to do the difficult things for Jesus like share our faith, clean the church kitchen, and serve the homeless at the annual soup kitchen service day. But Jesus meant something much more dire. He meant you'd have to risk being executed as a criminal of the state to follow him, or that you would have to risk giving up your identity, being abandoned by your friends and family, and losing everything.

Today we think of the cross as decoration.

Diluted.

When Jesus was alive, the Romans lined Jewish roads with crosses and murdered Jews on them for opposing Rome. Blood. Death. Murder. The cross meant death, a particularly shameful and wretched death.

"Take up your cross and follow me," Jesus said. That's crazy. No wonder we come up with new interpretations of that today, because it seems the original meaning is hazardous to church-growth philosophy. No wonder we dilute this down. We certainly don't like the idea of co-crucifixion.

The message of Jesus is not very seeker friendly. These ideas don't often produce big churches with big budgets. But do we even recognize the real message anymore? Or have we become so used to the diluted message that the real stuff seems too harsh, too real, too difficult? Have we gotten to a place where we don't even want the real message? Maybe we like our diluted versions better.

THE TEMPLE

The truth is that Jesus was not really seeker friendly. It seems he didn't really care what anyone thought of him or whether anyone followed him. He was on a mission from God, and he was going to fulfill that mission.

At one point, which may have been the straw that broke the camel's back, Jesus walked into the temple and opened a can of crazy on everybody there. This scene, Jesus clearing the temple, is central to this book. So let's back up and get the whole story so we don't miss it.

A week before his crucifixion, Jesus rode into Jerusalem, the capital city, on his Harley . . . well, that's what we like to think here in Milwaukee. Let's at least pretend his donkey's name was Harley. It was Passover week, and the streets were probably abuzz with activity, filled with crowds of tourists coming to celebrate Passover from all over the region. And then Jesus rolled into town. People had heard of him; maybe some had even seen him perform a miracle. Many people thought he was the deliverer, the Messiah King who would lead a successful rebellion against the Romans and establish Jewish dominance over the world.[4]

And so the people cried, "Hosanna!" Literally, "Save us, please." Jesus, save us! Save us from the oppressive force of the Roman occupation! We are desperate for a deliverer! Please, Jesus, please!

They were ready to crown him king. To follow him into a rebellion. But Jesus had other plans.

Can you imagine the scene? The people were poised to make their move. When would Jesus do it? Today? Tonight? The moment was ripe with anticipation for a coup. The leaders, both Jewish and Roman, would have been on high alert. What better time to lead a rebellion than Passover, when the city was full of Jewish peasants starving for freedom.

First stop: the temple. The temple was not just a church. It was the center of Jewish life—their religious devotion, their thought life, even their politics.

Imagine if city hall were not only the political headquarters, but also the university and church headquarters as well. All in one. Unified power. That is what the temple was in Jesus' day.

But something had gone terribly wrong in the temple. It had lost its mission, vision, and purpose. It had descended into a pyramid scheme rather than the center of worship for the God of all creation. The religious leaders were getting rich on side deals and kickbacks with the Romans, all the while embezzling temple funds, offering it as a market to the highest bidder.

This was oppressive to the people. The Romans were using the temple to proclaim their politics and even at one point erected a statue of Caesar there! The temple taxes were so high that the people were suffering. So not only did the Jews have to pay the Roman taxes; they had to pay the temple tax as well. They watched the temple leaders pull up in their Bentleys, wearing their Armani suits, while regular farmers watched their children die because they couldn't afford to buy food.[5] The injustice of profit and power replaced holiness as the cloud that hovered over the temple.

Jesus was coming to confront this injustice head on. It was oppressing the people, and it was about to come crashing down. Brick by brick. The stage was set for a showdown!

Here is what the Scriptures say: "On reaching Jerusalem, Jesus entered the temple courts and began driving out those who were buying and selling there. He overturned the tables of the money changers and the benches of those selling doves, and would not allow anyone to carry merchandise through the temple courts. And as he taught them, he said, 'Is it not written: "My house will be called a house of prayer for all nations"? But you have made it "a den of robbers"'" (Mark 11:15–17).

The selling of animals and money changing was actually a legit activity. People coming from all over the region could not pack their lamb or whatever they would sacrifice with them on this long journey. So the merchants were offering the travelers a service, a convenience. Also, the currency Jews were required to use in everyday life was Roman currency with Caesar's image on it, but this currency was considered pagan and could not be used to pay the temple tax. So the travelers would need to exchange their Roman coins for Tyrian coins to pay the required temple "tax" or required offering.

This was all legit, even needed in some ways. But Jesus would have none of it. In John's gospel, it says he formed a whip and drove all the livestock out. Jesus formed a whip. Just let that image roll around in your mind for a while. Jesus drove everyone out with a whip.

So why was Jesus so upset?

Yes, the merchants and religious leaders all were in cahoots, giving each other kickbacks.[6] But there was something else going on here. The merchants could have set up outside the temple. But instead, they set up their tables in the outer court, which was the place of worship for outsiders, non-Jewish converts. So the outsiders had no place to worship God. Their place of worship was taken up by vendors. Remember Jesus asked, "Is it not written: 'My house will be called a house of prayer for all nations'"? (Mark 11:17).

All nations. Outsiders. Insiders. Everyone.

The leaders had excluded the "all nations," and Jesus would have none of it. This was injustice, and Jesus would not let it stand. So he turned over the tables of injustice and drove out everyone with a whip.

Today, who are we excluding from worship?

Remember city hall, the one that was also the church headquarters and the university office? Imagine walking into the city hall of a major city, but the mayor was also the pope and the president of a prestigious university. So you stroll into the mayor/pope/president's office and start turning over tables, opening file cabinets, pulling out files, and throwing them into the air, turning over computer screens onto the floor. You even knock over the coffee and doughnut stand! Imagine leaving the place in complete chaos and destruction, and then you say as you leave, "This place is going down—it's a hall of corruption and injustice, and I'm going to bring it down."

You'd be marked. People would be out to get you. And if you lived in Jesus' day, you'd be killed. Because threats to the system were eliminated. Threats to the system could not be allowed to remain.

Mark says it this way: "The chief priests and the teachers of the law heard this and began looking for a way to kill him, for they feared him, because the whole crowd was amazed at his teaching" (Mark 11:18).

If you were a follower of Jesus, this would certainly have been exciting to witness. Jesus confronting the injustice of the temple system. Jesus putting everyone in their place. But I imagine a realization or two would soon set in: This guy is dangerous. He is going to get killed. And we might get killed with him. We are risking our lives following him. Jesus is putting our lives in danger.

This is a book about risk. This is a book about proximity. Moving into the neighborhood, taking risks to follow Jesus into the dangerous places in order to confront injustice and every human-diminishing activity.[7]

God became a man and dwelt among us. God did not stand off far; God came near. God saw us, heard us cry out in our oppression, and God moved down into our neighborhood in order to save us. Took up our lives, took up our pains, took up our brokenness, and declared to the powers that held us in bondage: "Enough! Let my people go!"

God turned over the tables of injustice.

Kids should not have to eat orange peels, and the only way anything will ever change is if we move our lives closer to the hurting, stand before the systems of injustice, and turn over their tables. To do that we are going to have to get close. To do that we are going to have to change our proximity. To do that we are going to have to make intentional decisions that cost us something.

We are being called, as followers of Jesus, to make a whip out of cords and turn over the tables of injustice in our world. That may cost us something. We may have to sacrifice our dreams.

That's risky. That's dangerous. But God is a dangerous God, and we are called to be a dangerous presence.

This is not an easy book to read. This book will hurt. It will strike deep into the heart of your fears and your notion of the American dream. It is not seeker friendly and probably won't make your church bigger. It might even make your church smaller. What makes this all the more remarkable is that nothing in this book is new. It has all been said before. Just open your Bible and start to read. It's all there. Sometimes we just don't see it, because we've covered up the real message with a more reader-friendly message.

The hope of this book is to say the things that have been said once all over again, to help us remove the counterfeit coating from the message of Jesus, and to take a deep bite into the true, authentic, dangerous message of the resurrected Jesus.

I hope you will join me on this journey. It is risky. It is dangerous. But following Jesus has always been life-threatening. Jesus once said, "Whoever tries to keep their life will lose it, and whoever loses their life will preserve it" (Luke 17:33).

STILL LIMPING

Here I was. I had given up my time and money to come and work with these hurting children in Russia eating orange peels. I was horrified at their living conditions. I was shocked that they had to eat orange peels. I knew in my heart that this was injustice and they should have a better life. But what could I really do about it? I was just one young guy standing in the face of tables and tables of oppression. So I justified it all in my head. I twisted the story. I worked some PR magic for the office of my ego. After all, I felt good about myself. I was doing something useful with my life, serving the kingdom of God by playing games with orphans. I spent a lot of money to get there. Took time out of my life to go and serve there. I was something else! I would go home and everyone would celebrate me for the amazing decisions I was making with my life. I would be a hero at home and on my campus. I was a *missionary*. I couldn't wait to get back and tell my story. I wanted that attention. I wanted that fame. The kids would give me a good story to tell my friends. They too would be amazed. They would "ooh" and "ah" and say, "Poor children," and I would spin it and make it sound like I saved their lives.

It was all a lie. Every bit of it. The whole thing was all about me. But I didn't realize this then. It took several years for me to realize all of this. I didn't realize I had been hit with a boulder. I didn't realize I was being called to change my proximity. I didn't even know that seeing the children eating the orange peels had any effect on me. This was how deeply blind I was. So self-absorbed.

But then one day I noticed I was limping. This limp was so annoying! "God, why do I have this nagging feeling inside of me? Why am I limping around like something happened to me? Why do I see injustice all around me now?"

Then it was all made clear.

I had been hit with a boulder from heaven that broke something inside of me that caused me to limp on that day. I had lost my blindness, but only now realized I could see.

Then I remembered the orange peels. It all began at the orange peels.

Like peeling back the fabric of time, my mind tumbled from one thought to another. Then I realized something even more disturbing, but we'll get to that later.

For now, I'd like to introduce you to Bob.

2

WHAT ABOUT BOB?

I have a friend whose name is Bob. He is older than most of my friends. At seventy-five, he has a passion for engaging in systematic issues of oppression in the city.

One morning I was having breakfast with Bob at George Webb's Restaurant. He told me something profound that I don't think I will ever forget. Bob has made a lot of money in his life, working his way up to CEO for a retirement community. He knows what success looks like in the business world.

Bob told me, "I have spent my whole life doing what I wanted to do and asking God to bless it. I'm tired of living that way. I want to start doing what God wants me to do."

After I finished seminary[1] and spent a year on the mission field, I found myself in a small Wisconsin town about thirty minutes outside Milwaukee working as a youth pastor. This is where I learned I was not called or equipped to work with youth. It was a hard lesson to learn, but valuable. About a year into that gig, I was asked to start a new church in Milwaukee. I was happy to do this. It sounded pretty exciting and, in reality, I needed a new job.

So my pregnant wife and I, along with our four-year-old son, packed up our bags and moved to Milwaukee. This was a new adventure for us. For many years, I had thought it would be great to plant a new church, and here was my opportunity!

We bought a house in the city. I did all the demographic work, because that's what all the church planting books tell you to do. We found the perfect location, and I was excited. We were going to start a super-cool, urban church that attracted young urban professionals and their families. We would have lots of people wearing skinny jeans and dark-rimmed glasses, have lots of tattooed, coffee-drinking, indie-music-loving twentysomethings. Our worship music would be amazing. We would grow quickly and become one of the biggest churches in the Milwaukee Metro. *Outreach* magazine would be writing stories about us, and I'd be invited to speak at conferences around the world, sharing the secrets to our success. Why? Because I was the pastor, and I had the vision, baby!

You might laugh. Are you laughing? Smiling? Smirking?

Why?

This was my dream. This is what I longed for, dreamed of, and wanted with all the depths of my soul. I was completely and absolutely seduced by the idea of "pastor celebrity." And I wanted it.

This was my dream.

I was strangely optimistic, which actually doesn't suit my personality. I don't see a glass half full or half empty, the glass simply has water in it—so either drink the water or pour it out. I like to call myself a realist which this is what pessimists call themselves to make themselves feel better.

It didn't take long for me to see that things were not going to work out like I had hoped. This was harder than I had imagined.

Reality quickly set in. Things weren't going well . . . at all. My dream was dying.

We barely had any money. As a side job, I began to work at the church where I used to be the youth pastor—as the janitor. I cleaned the church where I once was a pastor. Cleaned the toilets. Cleaned the youth room of the kids I once led. I appreciated the job, and the church was gracious in allowing me to do it. It was a bit awkward.

But it gets worse.

Our church plant was what people in the church planting world call a "parachute drop." The image describes it pretty well. I was dropped in with little money and no resources. I didn't know the city, and I didn't know anyone.

Did I mention that I grew up in the South? More specifically, I grew up in rural Appalachia.[2] This makes me a hillbilly. Have you ever seen that show on The Discovery Channel called *Moonshiners*? Those are my people! I was a Southern hillbilly living in the Brew City.[3] Every time I went anywhere and opened my mouth, people would say, "You're not from around here, are you?"

A church planter's job is to meet people. Do you know those people in the grocery store who have already had six conversations by the time they're standing in line to check out? They have milk and eggs and know the life story of three people, two of whom they led to Jesus on the spot. All in fifteen minutes.

Those people are church planters!

Well, I'm not one of those people.

When I go into the grocery store, I keep my head down, get what I need, and get out of there as fast as I can. I don't speak to anyone. Ever. It's not that I don't like people. I do. I'm just a bit quiet, a bit socially to myself. I think and process internally. I'm an introvert. People think introverts are shy, but we aren't really shy. We just don't have a lot to say until we have something to say.

I should have been an engineer, or maybe a lawyer. But a pastor? A church planting pastor?

Things weren't going well. We didn't know anyone. I had a hard time meeting anyone. I was "not from around here." We had no money. I was working as a janitor to support my family. We had a four-year-old and a newborn.

We began "meeting," if that's what you want to call it, in a stand-alone movie theater in our target demographic area. The name of the cinema was the Rosebud Draft House and Movie Cinema. This place was super cool (remember what I was going for), and instead of regular theater seating, it had velvet loveseats.

When you came to church, you got to sit on couches. This might seem cool at first, but then you realize that it's pretty early on a Sunday morning, and people are sitting in a dark cinema on a velvet love seat. Needless to say, people had trouble staying awake for the sermon.

In its infancy, Transformation City Church was already dying. It was a failing experiment. We were going to be another statistic of a failed church plant. But, honestly, I wasn't quite as worried about the future of the church as I was about the future of me. If Transformation City Church failed, that meant I failed. The word we use for people who have failed is *failures*. This doesn't look good on a résumé and certainly doesn't get my name published in *Outreach* magazine.

I was not going to be famous. I was not going to have a big church. No one would ever want to interview me. My dream was dead.

But although my dream was dead, the story was not. Things were about to change, but not in the way I expected them to.

I remember the moment of epiphany for me. I was driving. I had been praying a mix of laments ("Oh God, why is this happening to me? Where are you?") and deal brokering ("God, if you open up a door for another chance, I will serve you with all that I am"). Basically I was trying to make a deal with God to get me out of this terrible situation. The broke, failure, church-planter janitor wasn't what I wanted for my career trajectory.

I was trying my best to spin this story so someone else would hire me. But the problem was this: Remember that house I bought? Well, I owned it, and by this time, the proverbial housing bubble had burst. Pop. I was upside down under water in a three-bedroom bungalow in the city, and the housing market had collapsed. There was no way I was going to sell my house. I was stuck.

Have you ever had a "life flash in front of you" moment—when loads of information flash before you in an instant? You try to tell the story to someone, but it takes you ten minutes to explain what happened in that instant. Almost like a boulder falling from heaven. What do you say: "Boulders don't fall from heaven"? Well, they do where I'm from, and from the looks of it, they fall pretty often. That's why there are signs in the mountains that say, "Watch for falling rocks."

So as I was driving, all of a sudden I had this ten-minute conversation with God that took place in the span of .6 milliseconds. Instantly.

I came to this absolutely new place in life, a foreign territory I had never set foot on before. The land was called "surrender." In that holy moment, standing on that holy ground of surrender, I made a commitment to God. I said, "God, if this is where you want me, I will do it. I will go down with the ship. This is failing, and I don't know what I'm doing. I'm a failure, and I failed. My career is over and my dreams are lost. I'm done. But I will see it through. If it fails, I will fail with it. I'm yours and this church is yours. Do with us what you desire."

My dream was dead. My self-centered dream of self-glorification was gone. All I had to look forward to were the dirty toilets.

I decided I'd follow Jesus into this hard place he was leading me. Into the place of failure. I had been asking God to bless my dream for my life that involved lots of accumulation and self-glorification. It was time I started to live *God's* dream for my life, which was going to be a lot harder.

Looking back on that moment, so many things happened that I did not even realize till later. I had a Jacob moment. I had been living for myself in a delusion of my own making. For so many years, everyone around me had been filling me with stories of how great I was, and I had come to believe it all. I was living in the story of my own making where I was the central hero. I had replaced Jesus as the Messiah of my own life.

I wrestled with God. Jesus came down from heaven and wrestled with me and asked me, "What is your name?" I replied, "My name is the Great Jason Butler." We wrestled a little more until I was exhausted and confused. I had been beaten down, and, lacking energy to stand any longer, I lay on the ground as Jesus looked me in the eye once more and asked me again, "What is your name?" This time I replied honestly with tears running down my face. I said, "My name is Failure; my name is Liar; my name is Self-Glorification." I was addicted to my own glory, and I needed a beat-down.

Jesus then looked into my eyes with compassion and said, "No, your name is no longer Jason. Your name is Servant."

As I got up to walk away, I noticed something had changed. No, not something . . . everything.

Shortly after that prayer I heard something I had not ever heard before. I heard the cry.

THE CRY

I love the book of Exodus. For me, it's what Genesis is pointing forward to and the rest of the Hebrew Scriptures are pointing back to. Now, I'm not saying Genesis is not important. It's essential. There would be no Exodus if there were no Genesis. I love Genesis. But I love Genesis because it gets me to Exodus.

Those stories of Abraham, Isaac, Jacob, and Joseph—they get us to Egypt. And Egypt is where the action is. Exodus 3 is where the story really begins to take shape. And it begins with a colossal clap of thunder dropped on the uncovered heads of humanity. It begins with a cry and God's response to that cry. The cry that inaugurates history.[4]

The cry that moves God.

Here was Moses, an exiled, adopted Egyptian with Jewish parents, living as a shepherd, trying to forget his past, creating a new identity in the middle of the desert. He almost got away with it. He almost lived his life out in peace—but not quite. God had other plans. So Moses climbed up the mountain one day to investigate some strange light and found a bush that was burning but not being consumed. Then his life was altered when, from that bush that was burning but not really burning, the voice of God spoke:

> I have indeed seen the misery of my people in Egypt. I have heard them crying out because of their slave drivers,

> and I am concerned about their suffering. So I have come down to rescue them from the hand of the Egyptians and to bring them up out of that land into a good and spacious land, a land flowing with milk and honey—the home of the Canaanites, Hittites, Amorites, Perizzites, Hivites and Jebusites. And now the cry of the Israelites has reached me, and I have seen the way the Egyptians are oppressing them. So now, go. I am sending you to Pharaoh to bring my people the Israelites out of Egypt. (Ex. 3:7–10)

Some scholars say this is the most important passage in Scripture because it reveals to us that God hears the cry of the oppressed.

God hears the cry. Your cry. My cry. The cry of the starving in Africa. The cry of the trafficked thirteen-year-old in Cambodia. The cry of the wife who has lost her husband. The cry of the mother who has lost her child.

God hears the cry. That changes everything. We don't even need to go further from there. We don't need any more words of the story. We have all we need. God hears. God sees. God is listening. Your cries have reached heaven's ears. The Creator, the Sustainer, the one who is and is yet to come. The Creator of all that is has heard your cries.

But it says more, because Yahweh goes on and says, "I am concerned about their suffering. So I have come down to rescue them" (Ex. 3:7–8).

God coming down to engage with the injustice that is being laid upon the people. Heaven crashing into earth. God coming down. This is incarnation language. God moving closer. Changing proximity. Getting involved in the messy, ugly business of deliverance. Because that's what God does. God moves closer, not farther. God acts and doesn't sit still. God hears.

The Creator moves, and when the Creator moves, there are consequences. There are implications to God's movement. When God moves, people go free. Oppressors are broken, and new worlds burst into reality. In this situation, God's movement was good news for the Jews and really bad news for Pharaoh.

But deliverance always comes in the flesh. History wasn't quite ready for God's flesh yet. That would come later in the story. So in order to bring about the deliverance, God chose Moses. The response to the cry was taking on flesh—Moses' flesh. Deliverance always needs flesh, remember that.

So here was Moses. He once lived in Egypt and was raised in Pharaoh's household. Moses wasn't in line for the throne of Egypt. But still, he was "in the house" somewhere. Moses knew the inner workings of Pharaoh's house. He had seen the oppression from the inside. He had dined at the tables of abundance while the slaves of Israel had made bricks. He was once the beneficiary of the exploitation of a group of people. Taking their lives, passion, and energy and putting it at the table of Pharaoh to be consumed. He knew how ruthless Pharaoh was.

That's why he fled Egypt in the first place. He was fleeing the wrath of Pharaoh. And now here he was, tending his sheep in the middle of nowhere. Just an average day, tending sheep, when God showed up in a bush that didn't burn, but was burning, and spoke to Moses.

Do you ever wish God would just speak to you and tell you what you should do? Like this?

Maybe you should be careful what you wish for. Just look at my interpretation of what God asked Moses to do: "Moses, I want you to go to the most powerful man in the known world, the leader of the nation that is rich beyond measure, has the fear of every nation in this region, to the one who all of Egypt considers god and say to him, 'This God whom you have never heard of demands that you let the slave labor that is building your kingdom and generating immense wealth for you and your nation, the slave labor that generates fame and fear from the whole known world, let them go. Pharaoh, who kills whomever you wish whenever you wish, let your slave labor go free!'"

Have you ever read it that way before?

Then Moses responded, "Um . . . God, you know, I'm kinda busy out here tending my sheep. My calendar is kind of booked up. Can you find someone else? You know, I don't speak all that well; I'm not your guy. You've made a mistake here. You need to find someone else." But what he probably really wanted to say was: "God, there is no way I'm going to Pharaoh and telling him this. He will kill me! There's no way he will agree to this; it's a lost cause. I've seen what he can do, and I know he'll kill me right there on the spot in front of everyone."

Moses was scared stiff. God was asking him to risk his life. To walk into the mouth of the dragon. To risk everything. To give up everything. This was a death sentence.

So, are you sure you want God to speak to you from a burning bush? Maybe you should rethink that.

Let's recap: God heard the cry. God came down. God came closer. But deliverance needs flesh and Moses was the one to deliver the message. The message could not be delivered from afar. It needed to be delivered up close.

Proximity.

God heard, sent Moses, and the history of the world was altered. God said, "This is my world and my people. Pharaoh, this is not your world, and you are not in charge. I'm taking my people back, and there's not a thing you can do about it. So get out of the way." A people was birthed and God's story began, and we are participants in that story even today.

Because God hears, God comes down and sends us to declare to the pharaohs of this world, "Let my people go!" Maybe there are all sorts of burning bushes around you, but you just can't see them because you don't want to see them.

Standing before Pharaoh is never easy, and he will never let his slaves go without a fight. It's a risky adventure for us. It may cost us more than we'd like to give. But as Richard Rohr so eloquently said, "Life is not about you, it's about God."[5]

FOLLOWING JESUS INTO THE CITY

I gave up, I cried, I quit, and in that moment, everything changed. I realized my career was over, that I had no chance of being someone. I was a janitor and a failing church planter. My career was over, my finances would probably fall apart, and I might end up in foreclosure.

In that moment, I started following Jesus.

For so many years, I had been listening to the voices promising personal success. When those noises were finally silenced, things got very quiet. I heard something new, something I had not heard before: the cry of my city, the cry of the oppressed, the marginalized, the enslaved. And when I heard that cry, it overwhelmed me in such a way that I could not hear anything else.

I realized that God had heard this cry all along. That God had been hearing prayers of suffering from the people living in this ghetto of poverty and despair all along.

Everywhere I went, I heard the cry. It invaded my soul.

Success, fame, career—they no longer mattered. What mattered was joining Jesus in the restoration of our city. To fight injustice. To move. To change my proximity.

I had to fail to hear the cry. I had to hit bottom to hear the cry. The voices of personal success and prosperity are loud, and they will drown out the cry of the oppressed. They had to fall apart in me, be silenced, so I could hear something new.

Jesus was moving into the city. I was going to follow him. I had left a bunch of Russian kids once and pursued my own dreams, and I learned something from that. I would not turn away again.

I knew from that point on that we would not be a cool church. Rather, we would be a church that lives to pour itself out for the benefit of the poor and oppressed living among us. We heard the cry, and our call was to deliver a message to Pharaoh: "Pharaoh, you dirty dog who exploits and enslaves. Your time is done here! Let God's people go!"

MILWAUKEE

We are in the midst of the greatest migration the world has ever seen—the migration from the rural to the urban. In Asia and South America, cities are growing at a mind-boggling pace as the promise of industrial jobs lures young people to the city in the pursuit of a "better life" than their farming parents. European cities are bursting at the seams as immigrants from northern Africa are migrating in search of a better life for their families. We are indeed in the midst of a massive global urban migration. This creates opportunities, but it also creates great problems for many cities as there simply are not enough jobs to fill the demand. This produces extreme urban poverty right alongside extreme urban wealth. But in America we are seeing something slightly different.

According to CNN, the top five fastest-growing cities in the US since the 2010 census are Charlotte, North Carolina; Raleigh, North Carolina; Cape Coral, Florida; Provo, Utah; and Austin,

Texas.[6] These are cities that are aggressively creating jobs for highly educated, young, business-minded workers. They are cities that, for the most part, have low poverty levels and generate great wealth. And if you look at the top ten list, all the fastest-growing cities in the US, with the exception of Provo, Utah, are in warm-weather, Southern states.

In America, we have cities that are growing rapidly, cities that primarily focus on finance and technology. These warm-climate finance cities are growing rapidly in the US, but we are not experiencing great urban growth as a whole in America. Rapid urban growth is selective, not seen in all cities in the US.

Why? Northern/Midwest, industrial-based cities are losing population at a staggering rate. In 1980 Detroit had a population over 1.5 million. Today that population has dropped below seven hundred thousand. Milwaukee, Cleveland, Buffalo—along with other postindustrial cities—have seen their populations drop rapidly as well. The common name for these cities is the "Rust Belt." The once dominant economies that produced high-paying jobs for immigrants and urban migrants through industrial jobs now lie in ruin, with populations fading, unemployment raging, and hope hard to come by.

In the 1970s, Milwaukee boasted the highest African-American wages per capita in the nation. Now, Milwaukee boasts one of the highest unemployment rates among African-American men in the nation, with some stats showing it as high as 55 percent.

In America, we have urban migration, but we also have urban population desolation. People aren't moving to all cities; there is a selection process. Some cities are left behind. Milwaukee is one of those cities, and it ranked as the fourth poorest city in America in 2011. Our graduation rate in the city is optimistically 50 percent. The infant mortality rate in the zip code that our church is in ranks as one of the worst in the nation, with levels equal to those of Botswana.

I could go on, but you get the picture. Our city is serving under the heavy hand of many oppressive pharaohs: unemployment, lack of education, racism, and injustice. People are leaving as fast as they can. Anyone with resources or money is getting out of the city, and it makes no difference the color of your skin. If you can get out, you are leaving. But let me make this distinction when I refer to "the city." I mean the central city or the inner city—whatever you call it. This is often different from "downtown." Our downtown Milwaukee is rather nice, urban, young, and artsy, with many universities and businesses. Our suburbs are booming with population, innovation, and growth. There is a similar story in other postindustrial cities. The downtown and suburbs are a stark contrast from the central city.

Why would anyone want to go there? I often get this image of a city where a war has broken out or the plague has been discovered. You have seen the movies, right? People pack their cars as fast as they can and get out of the city. They head for the refuge of the suburban or rural. This is what our postindustrial cities have experienced.

As everyone heads out as fast as they can, all that is left is the under-resourced population that the world has chosen to forget about. All that is left is a man-made ghetto. Things got hard, so people who could leave left. Churches left, too. How many stories have you heard about a church that used to be in the city, but over time the neighborhood "changed," and so the church sold the property and bought a new one out in the suburbs where "their people" now lived.

It's nice to serve the people who are easy to serve. To serve the people who look just like us. To serve the people we understand. The people who speak the same language or have the same cultural background as we do.

All across our nation, as people fled the cities for the safety and comfort of the suburbs, our churches followed. Shame on us! We had a God-given opportunity to stand up for what God stands up for—being part of the hurt and pain and uncertainty. But we left.

Sure, there are great stories of churches who stayed in the city—who refused to sell out to convenience, who embraced the changing demographics and served all people, even some who handed over the mantle of leadership to other cultures. But sadly those stories are rare.

We left the cities when they needed us the most. We ran away from the pain of our central cities. We still are.

Today, is there pain around you? Are you moving away from that pain or toward it? It will take much thought and intention to move toward the pain. Our natural reaction is always to flee. The strongest instinct is self-preservation, and it will take great strength of soul to put yourself second and the pain of others first.

Our calling is the same as Moses' calling: to stand up to the forces of injustice and oppression. Why? Because the people are crying out for help. They are crying out to God to be delivered.

So what does the city have to do with oppression? Isn't there oppression and injustice everywhere? Yes, there is. From rural Appalachian poverty to farmers suffering under the heavy hand of agribusiness, there is oppression. And we should be facing those forces of evil wherever they lie. But there is one thing we cannot deny: density.

Within our central cities, from Milwaukee to Detroit to Cleveland to Buffalo to Philadelphia to Washington, D.C. and on and on, our cities hold the largest populations of those who are suffering under the weight of oppression. Millions of people are suffering in our cities. Hunger is rampant. Education is lacking. Poverty is paralyzing.

THE DANGERS OF PATERNALISM

So let's pause for a moment before we get carried away and come to think that we are the new Moses coming to deliver people from their oppression. Let's make this distinction. We are just called to go stand up to Pharaoh; God does the delivering part.

If you are a white, middle-class American, then this is for you (I can say this because I'm white too): White people love to play Jesus. Sometimes, we think we are the saviors of the world. So we have to be careful here. We are not the savior. We need to avoid the dangers of paternalism.

Paternalism is "a policy or practice of treating or governing people in a fatherly manner, especially by providing for their needs without giving them rights or responsibilities."[7] Get that—providing for their needs without making them part of the process. This is the danger white people can fall into, because often when we talk about the city, we are talking about African-Americans and Latinos who are living in the city and the white people from the suburbs coming in to help.[8] This has its place, as we will see, but it is also a dangerous balance.

When I was studying missiology in seminary, I read an article by the leader of the Russian Orthodox Church. He outlined his problems with the Western Protestant church and why the Russian Orthodox Church had a rocky relationship with Protestant missionaries from the West. When the Soviet Union fell in the early 1990s, flocks of missionaries from America flooded Russia, planting new churches and establishing new ministries. Many missionaries who were working or preparing to work in Russia would say, "We are bringing Jesus to Russia."

Well, this statement, though usually well intentioned, did not go over well with the Orthodox Church because the Russian Orthodox Church was over a thousand years old. They had established churches in every village and city throughout Russia. They had history; they had authority with the people. They also had just survived one of the greatest persecutions of the church by any government in modern history. The Soviet Union tore down their churches, killed their priests, and imprisoned their faithful. The prior seventy years of their history were terrible, but they endured; they survived.

And then American missionaries began declaring, "We are taking Jesus to Russia." The Orthodox Church simply said, "No, you are not bringing Jesus to Russia. Jesus was here all along."

We face a similar danger when we talk about engaging our cities. The African-American church has been here all along, working diligently to serve the people, stand against oppression, and take care of one another in the name of Christ. So outsiders have to be very careful.

We need to see the struggles of the African-American and Latino churches in our cities to survive and thrive in the midst of poverty and neglect. We have to be very careful to not minimize their experiences or struggles. And we must remember that the white church has very rarely stood beside the black church in America. So we are viewed by many with skepticism.

Jesus has always been in the struggles of the African-American church, so we must remember that we are not the deliverer; Jesus is. We simply come to the city to partner with what God is already doing to set free and make new.

This is a difficult balance, one that takes time, one that has history, but one that we must walk nonetheless. I genuinely believe that our cities need those from outside the city to join them in their struggle against oppression and injustice, but not in a paternal way as to make this about "us" and "them." And also not in a way that just gives money but withholds presence.

This is why proximity is supremely important. We must live close to those who are hurting, invest our lives in theirs, listen to them, learn from them, allow their lives to speak to us, and allow them to invest in us. Then and only then we will see them for who they truly are: beloved children of God who have talents and abilities that we need to embrace.

The answer is not more money or stuff or government. The answer is more presence. Getting close. Allowing lives to intersect and both be changed forever. But to get close we must go, and to go we must hear the call, and to hear the call we must silence the voices of personal fame and success and be willing to be renamed "Servant." This is not hip. This is not cool. This is hard.

As everyone else flees from the pain of our cities, we are being called into the city. We are saying softly, "God has heard your cry. Jesus is here. He's been here all along. And because you are here and Jesus is here, we want to be here too. We will not leave you. We will stand with you, no matter what. We don't have all the answers, and we don't know how this will turn out, but we will stand with you against whatever oppressive force seeks to tear you down." We may lose something in this endeavor, but we may find something as well.

We have heard the cry and we cannot unhear it. So we must engage. This is how healing begins. This is how renewal starts—when we hear the cry and begin the journey of freedom. Yes, it will make us uncomfortable and push us to places we don't want to go, but the church is the carrier of the greatest message ever given to humanity—that God loves us so much that no barrier can stop his pursuit of humanity. No barrier can stop God from entering into every situation. Thus, as we are the carriers of this message of love, no barrier will stop us either. This is truly the way of life, the way of love, the way of freedom. It is the way of Jesus that will bring restoration to our lives and the lives of those around us. This is the Jesus way, the Jesus life, the Jesus truth. God's love is unstoppable.

So what about Bob and his desire to do what God wants him to do instead of merely asking God's blessing on what he wants to? Are you doing what you want to do and asking God to bless it? Or are you doing what God wants you to do?

3

RISK MANAGEMENT

Americans typically don't like risk. We see risk as bad, dangerous.

Risk can get us into trouble, ruin our finances, and mess up our future. Most of the time, we play it safe—in our finances, careers, and businesses. We may even pay people to be "risk managers." We are OK with some risk, but not much.

Some might point out that our whole economic system is based on risk—people investing with uncertainty on Wall Street. But remember that there is a difference between risk and greed.

It can be hard to see the difference sometimes, but the difference mean everything. *Risk* is the danger of losing something. *Greed* is the desire to gain more.

And in our view of the world—a worldview of scarcity—more is better and less is worse. Thus, while risk is bad, greed is very good (from that perspective).

Because of this matrix of fear, greed, and scarcity, American culture values safety above almost any other value. We want to keep our kids, houses, future, and retirements safe. We have become so obsessed with safety that we have produced a culture of fear.

Greed produces more stuff, which causes us to build walls around what we have so we will not lose it. After all, if there is only so much to go around, we can't afford to lose what we have. We become riddled with fear—always looking over our shoulder to what bad thing might happen—and that produces in us a desire to keep things as safe as possible. Our whole lives become centered on the motivation to keep things safe so we won't lose them.

Greed produces fear, and fear makes safety our primary objective. Just listen to the many voices telling you to be afraid, that your safety or the safety of your children is being threatened, and so in order to limit your risk you must ____________ (fill in the blank).

Politicians play on our fear when they tell us that our future, borders, finances, and very way of life are in jeopardy and so we must elect them to keep us safe. Corporations play on our fears when they tell us that we need to buy their products or some bad thing might happen to us. Advertisers tell us that we need to buy the car with new safety features or we may not survive the next car accident. The list goes on. Everywhere you turn, someone is trying to play on your fears to get you to elect somebody, give somebody or something more control over your life, or spend more money protecting something you might lose. The system is based on the fear of losing something.

Fear. Fear. Fear.

The Bible calls it "the way of the world." Don't conform to it. Repent of it. Renew your mind out of it. (See Rom. 12:2.) Sin is dangerous, but fear is like nuclear fallout.

Our culture is built to produce fear, and a curious question to ask is why. Why do so many try to play on our fears?

Because when we are afraid; we are paralyzed. When we are full of fear, we do not have the power to stand up to the powers of injustice. When we are full of fear, we maintain the status quo. When we are full of fear, we buy products, elect politicians, interact with others, and lead our families in such a way that is all about protecting who we are and what we have. Fear strips us of our power to change ourselves and the world around us and clouds our judgment of what is right and wrong. We may act or move, but in reality, we are not really acting or moving at all. We are stuck, paralyzed—and that's just how Pharaoh and every other power in this world wants it to be.

When we fear, we stop trusting God and try to take matters into our hands instead. Fear gets us to do some pretty weird things—like bomb other people and torture suspected criminals. Fear gets us to build fences and take medicine that we don't need. Fear messes us up and moves us away from living the life God intended. When we are full of fear, we are paralyzed. And that's just the way the world likes us to live—paralyzed.

But what is the root of fear? What is behind it all? Why do we fear? At its core, fear is a lack of trust. It is saying, "God, you don't care. You aren't here. You can't help. I don't trust you to provide, protect, make a way for me." Ultimately, fear destroys our capacity to love. It numbs our senses and buries our compassion.

Of all the terrible things in the world, of all the tools of Satan and the systems of the cosmos, fear is the worst. And yet, we bathe ourselves in the stuff. This is why the most repeated phrase in Scripture is "Fear not." Don't be afraid, because God is here.

When we fear, we move away. We build fences. We keep our kids in the house. Fear is destroying the world, because it is convincing us that God doesn't care, that God will not be with us. It is blinding us to our real purpose and destroying our capacity to love.

Fear is controlling us and producing the instinct of self-preservation above all other instincts. We can't give when we are holding on tightly. We can't give our lives away if we are protecting them. We can't give our stuff away if we are protecting it. To take risks, we have to take chances. We have to let go. We have to trust that, even though things look bad, God is present.

CLIMBING TREES

When I was a kid, I loved to climb trees. A few years ago, my family and I were back in the area where I grew up. Living in the city, we don't have a lot of trees, but the mountains of Virginia are covered with them.

My son was off playing somewhere by himself, using his imagination. Later, I saw that he was up in a tree, a little higher than I wanted my six-year-old to be. He hadn't seen me yet and my first instinct was to yell at him to get down because he might fall and break his arm. But I stopped myself. It took a lot of discipline to stay quiet. I reminded myself that he was a little boy, and little boys need to climb trees. They need to test their limits. They need to embark upon challenges all by themselves. They need a certain level of dangerous adventure. So I didn't say a word. I just watched. Sure, it was hard to watch. All I could think about was him falling and us heading to the emergency room to fix his broken arm.

Kids need to take risks. They need to push the limits. They need to learn what they are capable of.

It was such a pleasurable experience to watch my son navigate the branches and pull himself up. I could almost hear him thinking what his next move was. I could see when he was unsure of his footing and feared falling. It was a beautiful dance of him testing his limits and gaining confidence. It gave me great joy to watch my son learn what he was capable of.

After a while I went to him, while he was still in the tree. I calmly looked up and asked what he was doing. He looked at me like I was an idiot and said, "I'm climbing a tree, Dad."

Kids are blank slates. If we teach our kids to fear, they will play it safe. If we teach them separation, they will divide. If we teach them animosity, they will hate.

My son was just fine that day. Yes, he could have fallen, but I don't want to be overprotective of my kids. I want to let them test the boundaries of this world and figure out what they can and cannot do. I will be there if they fall to pick them up. But sometimes a kid just has to fall.[1]

If we don't take a risk, we will never have any stories to tell. And I'm afraid that we are becoming a culture with no stories to tell.

SOUTH BEACH

When LeBron James, one of the all-time basketball greats in the making, came out of an Ohio high school, the Cleveland Cavaliers made him their first round draft choice, giving hope to an entire city. During his time in Cleveland, LeBron led the Cavs to conference championships and just barely missed an NBA championship. But when his contract expired, he was ready for a change. There was intense speculation about where he would choose to play next. Every team wanted him. Every team was an option for him.

With much fanfare, LeBron called a press conference to announce "the decision." During an ESPN interview, he boldly declared to the sporting world, "I'm taking my talents to South Beach." In other words, he had chosen to play for the Miami Heat.[2]

From Cleveland to Miami. From one of the poorest cities in the US to one of the richest beach fronts it has to offer. I mean, what would you choose? Cold, dark, dreary Cleveland (sorry Cleveland) or South Beach?

My point is not to criticize LeBron's decision. I just want to point out how LeBron's decision reflects our common desire for increased quality of life.

There are exceptions, but when we decide where to work and live, most Americans focus on quality of life. We are the epitome of a mobile society—no longer bound by hometowns or home states. We can go wherever we want; and the appeal of living in a warm climate, where there are lots of activities and a high quality of life is too appealing for many to pass up.

Remember the list of fastest-growing US cities? Almost all of them are in warm climates. Warm climates offer year-round activities. We don't have to scrape snow and drive on roads of ice. We can go boating, kayaking, and hiking all year round. If we had our choice, why wouldn't we choose warm climates to live in? Warmth helps us flourish.

And people have always desired to flourish. But what does this mean? For some ancients, it meant having enough food to eat, shelter, and ways to provide for basic needs. Over time, flourishing has come to mean different things to different cultures. In America, flourishing no longer means just having our basic needs met; flourishing is about satisfaction of life.

In his book *A Public Faith*, Miroslav Volf says, "For many in the West, experiential satisfaction is what their lives are all about. It does not merely enhance flourishing; it defines it."[3] This seems to be true, doesn't it? The satisfaction we have with life defines our lives and defines and informs our ideas about what it means to flourish. Individual, experiential satisfaction equals human flourishing.

We want to make more money to have a better life. We want to live in a city or suburb that meets our needs. We want to enjoy life, so we invest in those things that give us enjoyment—whether that's sports, outdoor activities, or vacations. Flourishing today means feeling satisfaction with our lives. Many of us don't really worry about basic needs anymore; we have those covered. Those are standard. We can pick those up at Target. Now, we seek to enhance our lives to feel satisfied. Satisfaction is our life goal.

But something happens in this pursuit of satisfaction. We forget about one major component of our satisfaction—our soul's satisfaction. Not the outer, skin-deep satisfaction of our job, climate, or what we are doing this summer, but something deeper, something more, something primitive even—our human need for love. To give love and to be loved.

The more we focus on our satisfaction, the more we focus on ourselves. The more we focus on the pursuit of the best life for ourselves, the less we focus on love. Because love is sacrifice. Love is putting others before ourselves. Love is impossible without thinking about another person, sacrificing for the other.

Again, Volf says, "When the scope of love diminishes, love itself disappears; benevolence and beneficence mutate into the pursuit of self-interest. Something similar happens to hope, which is understandable if hope is love stretching itself into the future of the beloved object. . . . So when love shrinks to self-interest, hope disappears as well."[4]

Self-interest is incompatible with love. By definition, they oppose one another. When self-interest increases, love decreases; and when love increases, self-interest decreases. Love seeks the benefit of the other, not the self. Self-interest and love are like oil and water; they just don't mix.

Maybe that's why hope is hard to find—because love is hard to find. But self-satisfaction is everywhere.

Love will cost us something; love *always* costs us something. It is always a giving of ourselves. Love requires that we open ourselves up to others, to be vulnerable, and then give something of ourselves away.

Love is what God commands of us—not the pursuit of satisfaction, but rather the pursuit of love.

Late in his life, Jesus told his disciples, "Guys, listen. You will be known by how you love. People will know you by your love, by how you give yourselves away" (John 13:35, paraphrase). Maybe this is why fewer and fewer people know about Jesus in America. Why so many people have become disillusioned with the church and Christians. Because we've become consumed with self-satisfaction and have forgotten how to love.

If the world should know us by our love, what does it mean when they don't know us? It means we've failed to love. All we can see is ourselves. We live in a hall of mirrors where we can't see past ourselves to the needs of others.

I heard an interview on National Public Radio the other day with a researcher who studied the balance between the amount of time people have to wait in an elevator with the number of elevators available. She said people are generally willing to wait for twenty seconds in an elevator before they become restless. When the interviewer asked what people do if the wait is longer than twenty seconds, she said something like, "We have found that if the wait time is too long, we can install mirrors in the elevators and people will not notice the wait."

Funny. We like looking at ourselves. We like to look in mirrors because we are self-absorbed. We look to see if things are right, if anything is out of place, because we want people to think good thoughts about us. We are afraid that our lives will not live up to the standard of self-satisfaction we have predetermined. We mostly seek our own benefit, and that is why the church in America is shrinking.

Love demands risk, seeking the benefit of the other above ourselves. It demands sacrificing our hopes and dreams and putting others' hopes and dreams before our own. It means sacrificing what I have and who I am for the benefit of another. Isn't this what the cross is about?

When we make wedding vows, this is the covenant we are making—to love one another. To put each other ahead of ourselves. To seek the benefit and the blessing of the other above ourselves. When I counsel people who are struggling in their marriage, I ask, "How are you putting your spouse's needs above your own?" Usually, they are silent. That's why their marriage is suffering. They've forgotten to love, to put the needs of the other before their own.

Self-satisfaction will destroy a marriage. It will do the same to a life. And it does the same to the church. Self-satisfaction is unhealthy to systems of covenant, and the way to health is through outward-focused, sacrificial love.

At a conference, an older gentleman told me about a church he was part of "back in the day" in Milwaukee. He said they were right in the heart of the city, but then they made the decision to move out of the city because the neighborhood changed. He looked down and said, "That was a bad decision." That decision killed the church.

When the church moves out of the city because the neighborhood is changing, it is just a matter of time until it falls apart. When the church spends millions of dollars on its audiovisual system and has little left over to engage the poor, it is just a matter of time until it falls apart. When the church worries more about the upkeep of its building than the neighborhood that is desperate outside of its doors, it is just a matter of time until it falls apart.

I believe that God cares more about the poor than our buildings or audio systems. Maybe we should too. Self-satisfaction has no place in the kingdom of God.

PINE BOXES

When I was in my twenties, I took several three-month trips to Russia to work with orphans, and after seminary—years after the orange peel experience—my wife (who is Russian) and I lived in Vladimir, Russia, for a year, teaching in a seminary and assisting the local church in a variety of ways.

The thing I disliked most about being a missionary was the language. They don't speak much English in Russia, and this was hard for me. My language-learning skills are on par with my ice-skating skills—not very good. Overall, the year we lived there was a nice time. I sometimes miss it nostalgically; I miss the culture and the hospitality of the people, the urgency of the mission, the food, and riding on those old Soviet trolley buses. Sometimes we think of missionaries as "suffering for Jesus," and some certainly are, but I would not describe my time as life-threatening or difficult. Nor would I say that I suffered at all. It was nice. Russia is a nice place with lots of great people.

I know missionaries around the world. They are amazing people doing amazing things for the kingdom. But being a missionary is different now than it was a few hundred years ago. Most missionaries I know have pretty nice budgets, using funds they were required to raise before leaving—living expenses, travel, retirement, home stay, ministry funds, and re-acquisition funds. Skype and the Internet keep them in touch with friends and family, and airline flights make it possible to get home pretty quickly if needed. The most inconvenient thing I experienced as a missionary was trying to learn a new language.

Yes, I'm overstating things to prove a point. There are many missionaries risking their lives every day for the kingdom. Praise God for them! So please don't think I'm disrespecting missionaries.

But no matter where one is serving today, being a missionary today is not nearly the risk it used to be in the past. There are stories of missionaries who lived in the seventeenth and eighteenth centuries who would leave for the mission field and literally pack their belongings in a pine box—a coffin—because they knew they were never coming home. They realized they would be buried on the mission field.

There was no practical way to get back. Ships took months and months to make the journey. If you were a missionary during this time, you knew that if you got sick, you'd die. You'd never see your family again. You were putting your children in extreme danger of making them suceptible to illness. For some, encountering native tribes meant the possibility of being murdered. You left and never came back. You packed your belongings in a pine box, the box you would be buried in. You were risking everything for love.

That's our legacy. We come from a long line of those who risked their futures and their presents for God's mission: Abraham leaving his homeland; Moses going back to Egypt; Joshua heading into the unknown; Esther standing up to the king; Nehemiah going back to Israel; Nathan calling out David; Jesus walking to the cross; Paul bearing the marks of Christ. These were people who were willing to take a risk, who were not concerned by what they might lose, but motivated by what there was to gain. These were people who did not worry about their personal safety or their retirement account, but risked their lives in order to bear the love of God to others. A long line of people who knew that their decisions would not increase their quality of life, but rather make their lives much more difficult.

We come from a long line of risk takers, of great lovers, of those willing to put others in front of themselves, of those willing to pour themselves out for the benefit of others.

Where is that risk today?

In America we seem to have a disease. Some type of disease where we only think about ourselves. We pass it down to our kids. We teach it in our schools and universities. We see it on our television screens and read about it in our magazines. It's making us very, very sick. It tells us to get ahead, make as much money as we possibly can, live well, and retire better.

I see college students who have so much potential to change the world. So much ability and talent to creatively engage the problems and injustices in the world, but over and over again I see them settle for small stories. I see them settle for the best-paying jobs because they are afraid of their student loans, settle for the cool apartments in hipster urban neighborhoods because they are afraid of being left out. Then they have children and move to the suburbs where they can be safe because they are afraid their kids might get hurt or not be in the "best" school.

We settle for selfish, individualistic, small lives when God is calling us to live into a bigger story.

I firmly believe that the greatest perceived risk that Americans can take in our world today is moving into our urban inner cities—the core of our cities that are suffering from poverty, neglect, crime, and dysfunction. (Please don't think for a minute that it's the fault of those living in the inner cities. Nope, the people with all the power and influence left, and that sparked the cycle of poverty and neglect.) The hurting do not need our money, ideas, or solutions. They need us—in the flesh. They need our relationship, our listening ear, our hand on their shoulders. They need our presence, not our presents.

I have heard the stories of young people who tell their parents that God is calling them to be a missionary in a foreign country. Oftentimes that announcement is celebrated by their parents, church, and mentors. Sure, there is apprehension, but for the most part, there's joy that God is using their children.

I have also seen young people tell their parents that they are going to move into the hurting part of the city—to invest their lives in the pain, poverty, and brokenness of an under-resourced neighborhood.

The reaction is much different. The reaction I have seen all too often is one of horror and denial: "No, you can't do that!" "You can't go live with those people." "You are throwing your life away. Think of your future." "You could get killed there."

Our central cities are perceived as the most dangerous places in America. Highways bypass our central cities. Bus routes neglect them. Businesses and churches leave. People with resources get out. Gangs, pimps, drugs, crime—it all collects in the center of our cities, like a giant funnel of despair.

A fellow Christian who lives in the suburbs of Milwaukee told me that if one-hundred-dollar bills were lined up from the suburbs to downtown Milwaukee, he would stop picking them up at 108th Street. He said that he doesn't go any farther than that into the central city. Never mind the fact that he has another fifty blocks before he even gets close to the inner city.

This is the perception of American urban and under-resourced communities. Danger. Crime. Poverty. Drugs.

But the core issue is fear. Our own fear. We fear what we do not know, what we do not understand. We fear the differences we see in other people.

Our cities are dying and need hope, but there is no hope, because there is so little love. All there is a whole lot of the disease of self-satisfaction.

Our city, like so many other cities across the country, is a new mission field for a new generation. Not a mission field where we make quick converts, but rather a mission field where we invest ourselves and pour our lives out for the benefit of others. A mission field of love, sacrifice, commitment, and grace. A mission field of presence. It's a mission field where young college graduates are being called to take the risk of going to live and work, to teach at a "failing" urban school so kids can learn to read, to work as engineers and doctors and nurses and whatever else and live in an under-resourced neighborhood, to build relationships with families and kids and neighbors, to tutor and mentor, to live and learn, to listen and embrace, to love and serve, to use their resources and knowledge to stand up to the oppressive forces of poverty and discrimination, to use their talents to rebuild homes, to use their influence to remind city officials that the central city is part of the city too.

Yes, it's dangerous. Yes, it's risky. You might get hurt or robbed. It must be approached with wisdom and in partnership with a local church. You will need extreme amounts of humility, mentors and partners, and much, much prayer. It is the mission field for a new generation.

God has an epic story for you to embark upon. Don't live in the small story of self-satisfaction, which will only steal your soul and leave you sick and lonely. Live in the grand story of love, in the grand story of sacrifice.

You come from a long line of risk takers. Please don't settle for safety—take a risk for the kingdom of God. You were told that the world will know you by your love, not your pursuit of self-satisfaction. Let go. Embrace the life God has for you—the life centered around others and not yourself. Do that and you will have a story to tell, a story of redemption, a story of grace, a story of restoration.

You will lose much, but you just might gain everything.

4

ANYTHING GOOD

Right after Ben and Megan had been robbed for the third time, we all were sequestered in the kitchen. Two police officers poked through their personal belongings—the violation following the violation.

"My guess is it's somebody you know," one officer said.

"We know that," Megan said.

"We can dust everything they might have touched, but that probably won't prove anything. It's not like on *CSI*," he smiled.

Glancing out the window, I wondered how we could hire Ben and Megan. Recently, our neighbors had the "eco-friendly" idea of hanging tinsel on their outside bushes; within minutes the wind had strewn it over the street and our yard. Still, it sparkled pretty, provided you knew it was tinsel, and not sharpened razor blades, which, in this neighborhood, was a more reasonable conclusion.

"They didn't take the computer," the other officer said, peering into the dark monitor, as though it were a Magic 8 Ball that would give him an answer. Just then the screensaver started, a slideshow of Community House pictures: us smiling, neighborhood kids smiling, staff smiling, volunteers smiling; everyone smiling as though they had discovered a really good secret.

As the officers left, Megan thanked Kevin and me for being there. We shrugged and shuffled our feet, unsure of where else we should be but here.

Ben braced Megan from the back, his arms resting against her ribs, hands cradling their unborn baby. Last Christmas they had played Mary and Joseph. This Christmas they were not playing. Their baby would be born in the 'hood, in our stable of bachelors, in the awe of little wise kids. And her name shall be called Cadence Grace.

When one of the disciples, Philip, told his friend, Nathanael, that Jesus was from Nazareth, Nathanael exclaimed, "Nazareth! Can anything good come from there?" Philip smiled and responded, "Come and see." (See John 1:46.)

The above story was first told to me by Ben Parman, who lives in our "Community House." But let me back up. What is the Community House, and why were people being robbed?

When our church heard the cry of the city, everything changed for us. We couldn't get it out of our ears. We decided that the function of our church would be to engage the pain and brokenness of our city—to follow Jesus into the city and invite others to join us.[1] So we began to pray, "Lord, how do we engage the city? How do we follow you into the city?"

By this time, Tim Nelson had joined me on staff. Alone and broken, I had put out one last job posting, searching for someone to join me. I needed a co-laborer. The job posting went something like this: "Looking for an associate pastor to come and join a new church plant focused on bringing hope, healing, restoration, and salvation to the city. . . . At this time we cannot offer any salary compensation." I didn't get many bites on that one, except for Tim. He was working as the youth pastor for a big church in Alabama and his wife had a nice job working for the University of Alabama. They left their jobs and moved to the Milwaukee central city to work alongside us with the promise of no real paying jobs. It was a risky decision and dangerous for one's career. But now they have a story to tell—a big one. They relocated. Changed their proximity. And it changed their lives.

As Tim and I prayed about how we were to engage the city, we both heard the Spirit speaking to us and saying, "You have to live there. You have to have a permanent presence in the city." What did this mean? Our church was in the city. Our homes were in the city.

As we continued to pray, we began to form the dream of intentional living in under-resourced neighborhoods. "Intentional living" meaning that odds are no one would just decide to go live in the central city just because they wanted to. You would have to be intentional and deliberate in making your decision. You would realize it was not going to be easy, and the only way you would make it was to feel a call and a sense of urgency for the healing of broken lives.

After we prayed through this, and as the vision began to be birthed in our hearts, we knew what we needed to do. The church needed to buy a house in a hurting, under-resourced neighborhood.

Now you must understand something. "The church" that I speak of was Transformation City Church, and at this time we were twenty-five people at most.

How could a church so small buy a house? That question was irrelevant. The Spirit was speaking, and we wanted to listen. So we went looking for a house in a central-city neighborhood. This was at the dawn of the foreclosure crisis—there were plenty of houses. The real issue was finding a house that was capable of being fixed up. It had to be somewhat intact. Our realtor used the expression, "Tore up from the floor up." When a house is empty in the city, it gets pilfered—people break in and take anything of value, anything they can scrap or sell. Copper is the Holy Grail. They break walls to take out pipes, take water heaters, furnaces, and even pull out electrical wire. Sometimes the houses attract squatters or become temporary brothels.

It was hard to find a house that had hope. But we finally found one. If I showed it to you today and told you it had hope, you'd laugh. It was an abandoned, foreclosed duplex that was being squatted in and looked like it was being used as a drug house. But we loved it, so we bought it.

It was the biggest decision we had made to this point as a church. We had little money, and this took our whole budget.

This is not the typical first purchase for a small church plant. Some people were excited about it; others were not. A few people even left the church over it. They thought we were crazy. I think they were right.

We spent the next three months and seemingly every extra dollar of every person in the church to fix up that place. We pulled dumpster after dumpster of foul-smelling, rotted debris out of that place. Then we began to rebuild. We fixed it up, transformed it. After all, that's what we are about.

Now we had a house, but we needed people to live in the house. To live intentionally, to pour out their lives for the benefit of the neighborhood. In simple words—to love. To move there and build relationships with the neighbors, hang out with the kids, invite people over for dinner. To work normal jobs but then see their mission—their purpose—as investing themselves in the neighborhood. To live in community in a hurting community.

What we did not realize was that everything we had done so far was the easy part. Money—easy. Remodeling—easy. Finding people to live there—hard.

We knew that there were youth living in this neighborhood who needed someone to love them and pour their lives out for them. There were daughters with no dads and sons who couldn't read. There were kids who were valuable and had a future, but every system around them told them otherwise. In their schools, they were "behind." In politics, they were "takers." To the police, they were "criminals." But to God, they were "beloved."

We did not have any youth in the church yet, so we did not have a youth ministry. We decided that these kids were worth beginning a youth ministry. So we did the only thing we knew to do. We put out another post: "Exciting urban church with multiple staff in search of an urban youth pastor to live in an under-resourced community to build an urban youth ministry from the ground up within a church that desires to bring hope, healing, restoration, and salvation to our city. At this point we cannot offer any salary compensation."

A few months later, Kevin Sas (pronounced "sauce") joined us. He relocated. Changed his proximity. He came to live in a neighborhood that most people would say is "dangerous."

Kevin was the first resident in our Community House project. A white guy from Iowa whose grandfather is a corn farmer began living in an all African-American neighborhood.

He just lived there. He was asked a lot of questions like, "What are you doing here?" To be honest it's a little strange—a single white guy living in an all African-American neighborhood. He would sit on his front porch and wait for people to come and talk. The kids were the first ones to engage him. Everyone was skeptical, and we learned that trust takes time. There was no "ministry" going on, no witnessing, no helping—just living.

In the daytime, Kevin would make subs at an upscale sandwich shop in the financial sector downtown. In the evening, he would come home to the 'hood to hang out with the kids. Kevin loves games more than anyone I know, so he began playing board games and Xbox with the kids, throwing a football, and playing basketball.

The kingdom of God is like a mustard seed: things begin slowly, small. Like a quiet revolution. Kevin was planting a tree and watering that seed.

Remember, one must earn the right to be heard. One must earn trust. It is never given; it is always earned. Kevin was earning the right to live in this neighborhood, the right to be a voice, the right to be trusted.

He lived in the six-bedroom duplex for a while by himself. Then we noticed that there were a lot of kids in this neighborhood. So we decided we needed more people to invest in their lives.

Does your church staff for the needs of the church or for the needs of the community around you?

You know what we did? Yep. You know what the salary was? Yep.

Ben and Megan Westra joined us. They moved up from West Virginia. They had just married and decided that the first step they wanted to take on their life together was to move into an under-resourced neighborhood and pour themselves out for the pain and brokenness of others. Not your typical career path for success and prosperity . . . but maybe it is.

Fast forward a year or so later, and we're back to where we started. Ben and Megan had been robbed three times. Their house broken into twice. The car was stolen and totaled. They had known the cost of living in the central city, but this didn't ease the pain.

Now, most of us would have been afraid. Most of us would have decided this was not a safe neighborhood to have a baby in. Most of us would have left at this point.

But they didn't leave. They thought, "Other people had babies here. Why can't we do it?"

When Kevin, Ben, and Megan tell people where they live, people say, "Why do you live there? It's so dangerous! You have to move!" People get terrified for Ben and Megan's daughter. They say, "You can't raise your child there—she will not be safe."

But Ben and Megan see life differently; they see the world upside down. They see the blessing of those who are poor. They see the mourners being comforted, and they want to be part of what God is doing there. They are living out their faith in radically dangerous ways. They are putting their calling and their love for God and neighbor above the fear that pushes us to seek personal safety above all else. They are living with and among the under-resourced and finding that they are the ones being blessed. They are the ones learning. They are the ones being loved. Their lives are the ones being changed.

OFF A CLIFF

One of my favorite pieces of Scripture is Luke 4, where Jesus came back to his hometown to worship in the synagogue:

> Jesus returned to Galilee in the power of the Spirit, and news about him spread through the whole countryside. He was teaching in their synagogues, and everyone praised him. He went to Nazareth, where he had been brought up, and on the Sabbath day he went into the synagogue, as was his custom. He stood up to read, and the scroll of the prophet Isaiah was handed to him. Unrolling it, he found the place where it is written: "The Spirit of the Lord is on

> me, because he has anointed me to proclaim good news to the poor. He has sent me to proclaim freedom for the prisoners and recovery of sight for the blind, to set the oppressed free, to proclaim the year of the Lord's favor." Then he rolled up the scroll, gave it back to the attendant and sat down. The eyes of everyone in the synagogue were fastened on him. He began by saying to them, "Today this scripture is fulfilled in your hearing." (Luke 4:14–21)

Jesus was in his hometown; these people knew him when he was growing up. Usually when people knew you as a child, they always remember you as a child.

Jesus was also in the synagogue. He had gone to church to worship on the Sabbath. The custom in Sabbath worship was to read aloud the daily Scripture—much like our liturgy. Note, the scroll was handed to him. All indications point to the fact that Jesus didn't pick this Scripture; he just read it. Jesus didn't manipulate the circumstances. He just read the "verse of the day" from Isaiah, then he sat down.

I love that—he sat down.

In Jesus' day, the teacher sat down and the students stood up. Today, it's the other way around. Jesus sat down because he was teaching. Then he said, "Today this scripture is fulfilled in your hearing" (Luke 20:21). This text is Jesus' mission statement.

He came to do what? Proclaim good news to the poor.

What is good news to the poor? Ever been poor? Really poor? What do you consider good news? That you can go to heaven when you die? Nope, that's not good news for people who are watching their kids die of hunger. Good news is news that says you don't have to be oppressed anymore, that you can provide for your family, that you will have a meal to eat tonight. That hope is real and tangible. That's good news.

Jesus said, "To proclaim the year of the Lord's favor" (Luke 20:19). What is the year of the Lord's favor? It's the Year of Jubilee. The celebration of the fiftieth year when all debts would be released, all slaves would be set free, all land would be given back. The Year of Jubilee was a restoration to the original God-intended condition. (See Lev. 25.)

The people were amazed. Is this the Messiah? Could it be? I mean, isn't this Joseph's kid? There was probably some cynicism there, since everyone would have known Mary and Joseph's story, and I imagine no one was buying the whole "conceived of the Holy Spirit" line yet. So you can imagine how they would view Jesus. But they liked what they heard. Maybe this was the Messiah.

Have you ever noticed that every time people started praising Jesus, he would say something to infuriate them?

The people were getting excited about this mission of Jesus. People were thinking that maybe this Jesus would lead them as their king, that Jesus might unite the kingdom and be the new David. Then Jesus ruined their party. He told them two stories of how God moved through the prophets Elijah and Elisha. One story was about a widow from Zarephath and the other a leper from Syria.

Do you know the connection between these two people—the widow and the leper? They were outsiders, non-Jews. These two stories were about God working outside of the Jewish system, and Jesus seemed to be saying that this mission from Isaiah, this healing, this Year of Jubilee, was going to come to the outsiders.

Here is my paraphrase of the scene: Jesus said, "God is bringing to fulfillment the ancient promise of Isaiah for the restoration of the broken systems. The unfolding of the ancient Year of Jubilee is underway. Healing is flowing from God's hand over the land, and it's coming through me." The people were amazed at this and rejoiced. "God be praised."

But Jesus went on: "You have been the keepers of God's grace for generations and have become so focused on yourselves that you can't see God any longer. All you can see is your own reflection, and you are imploding. I am here to tell you today that God is on the move, and God is going to move whether you like it or not. If you can't see past your own self-interests to the needs and pain of the world, then you will miss it. You have a God-given destiny to be a blessing to the nations, to pour out the grace God has given you to the world. You were called to be restorers of the broken bridges, but you missed it. You have been focusing on yourselves for too long now. The only way you will find healing for yourselves is to bring healing to the nations. You are missing your calling!"

They didn't like this. But I can't blame them. I don't think I'd like to hear this either.

After they heard this, they tried to throw Jesus off a cliff. The message was so offensive to them—that God may be working outside of their systems, that God may be working among the outsiders, that God called them to live lives poured out instead of hoarding God's grace—it was so offensive that they tried to murder Jesus. Jesus was a threat to their view of the world. Jesus was a threat to their view of God. Jesus was dangerous to systems they had built over the centuries. And what do you do with threats? You eliminate them.

Church, we had better wake up and see that God's grace has been given to be poured out, that our lives have a destiny from heaven to bring healing and restoration to the outsiders, poor, broken, and prisoners. God is moving whether we like it or not, and we have a choice: either follow Jesus or get left behind. Our cities are full of suffering people of all ages and races, and the church can change the fortunes of our cities. But one thing is for sure—we won't change a thing if we keep thinking that God's grace is given for us to keep for ourselves, to hoard and store up in our bunkers of fear.

No. Jesus is bringing an end to the debts that have built up between us and God and between us and each other. Many of us are holding on to the deeds of debt and holding it against the poor and broken. We have the opportunity to rip up those deeds of debt and empty ourselves of our blessing. We still have that opportunity right now, but if we don't give them up willingly, they will be ripped out of our hands. We will lose the chance to partner with God to bless the world.

God is bringing restoration to the original God-intended condition. God is doing it whether we like it or not. We have the chance to join in, but we won't have that chance forever. Restoration is coming, and I think we should take the chance to partner with God while we still have it.

INHABIT

As we hang out around Transformation City Church, we get to see how God is working and moving in so many different ways, and the main reason we are witness to this transformation is because people are making intentional choices to pour their lives out for others, live in under-resourced communities, relocate and change their proximity, and take the risk of being robbed or have their car stolen.

The Community House has become the central component for how we engage our city as a church. We didn't realize it would be so important when we started; we were simply listening to the Spirit who told us to buy a house.

But this did not all happen overnight. Sometimes when we look back on history or our lives, we forget that the process was difficult and hard. We have revisionist tendencies. Everything we are doing here took time, energy, sweat, and blood. We don't sleep much, not because we are so busy, but because sleep is hard when there are so many moving pieces, so many thoughts, so many potholes to navigate on the journey. Every step has been difficult here as we constantly flirt with failure. Will this work? Most days we sat on the curb and prayed, "God, we have no idea what we are doing here. Help!"

It took time for the residents of the house to build trust with the neighborhood, because trust always takes time. They didn't do anything for a while but live there. They listened to their neighbors and played basketball. Imagine that—taking the time to simply be part of a neighborhood, to be accepted, to listen and learn. We so often want to fix things right away, but what we need to realize is that maybe *we* are the ones who need fixing and *others* have the solution to our problems.

As they simply lived, they began to see some of the neighborhood kids hanging around. Slowly, hearts started to open to them, and basketballs started to bounce.

After learning that Kevin, Ben, and Megan were pastors at a church (which was a bit of a secret for a while), one of the influential grandmothers who lived next door asked if the house would have some sort of Bible teaching for the kids. Bible Club was born. The neighborhood invited us to love their kids and we responded.

From then on, Bible Club has run every week, and in the summer, it is a half-day adventure that takes city kids to water parks, out to the country to pick apples, or to see movies, all while telling and showing them the love of Christ. All while showing the kids that they are valuable, good, worthy, beautiful, smart, talented, blessed, holy, grace-filled, funny, and wonderful.

From there, we began to connect people from our church to mentor and tutor kids in this neighborhood. One of the kids who was in the fifth grade could not read very well. This is injustice, and we would not let it stand. We connected a teacher from

Transformation City Church, who met with the student each week to study. A few of the kids loved art, but their art programs had been cut from their schools. So we arranged for a few artists from our church to teach them art once a week. There were kids who wanted to learn to play instruments—kids with great talent—so we connected some musicians with them to teach them to play the drums and guitar.

Last year we began praying again, "God, what is our next step with this Community House idea? What do you want us to do out of this?" We became restless; we knew God was stirring the waters of our souls. So we gathered a small group of people and began to pray and discuss the possible next steps for this ministry as a church. We had seen some amazing relationships form because of the intentional choice of people to move into an under-resourced ministry. We were reaching and impacting so many lives on so many different levels.

Please don't think that the only lives impacted were those living in the neighborhood. The Community House is like a radioactive fallout zone for transformation. You get close to it, and God is going to start moving in your life. If there was such a thing as a "grace Geiger counter," then when you came back from being around the house, the grace Geiger counter would be clicking and knocking; your grace radioactive levels would be off the charts. We send people from our church there just to "go see," and their lives begin to look different. They get close, and they get transformational fallout all over themselves. People from the church get involved in mentoring or tutoring, and their lives are changed.

Sometimes we think we are going to go be the blessing, but what happens is that we get blessed. We think we are going to teach something, but in the end, we learn more than anyone else.

We eventually began to see that this was the best thing about our church. That this was the place—ground zero for us—where God was moving and blessing. So we decided to reproduce it on a bigger scale. We would recreate this ministry house, not just once, but many times.

We launched a new nonprofit to stand beside our church with the specific purpose of recreating this Community House. We called it Inhabit. The mission of Inhabit is "to bear witness to the kingdom of God by recruiting Christians to intentionally live and serve in under-resourced Milwaukee neighborhoods." The vision is to buy foreclosed homes, fix them up, and then recruit individuals to live in these homes in order to intentionally serve the people of that neighborhood, pouring out their lives for the benefit of those around them. Through these relationships, we will tutor kids, mentor teens, hold Bible Clubs, teach art classes and music lessons, and more. Our dream was to have a network of five of these homes in five years in order to impact five neighborhoods for Christ by building life-changing relationships through intentional living.

That's a big vision. We realized it would be a lot of work. Our associate pastor, Tim, had a passion to see this vision birthed into reality, so we commissioned him to be the leader of the newly formed Inhabit. Our church would be down a staff person. Some thought this would be a bad idea and that the church would suffer.

We couldn't afford to give up a talented staff person. We are a growing church with lots of growing church needs. But this is where the Spirit was leading us. It has been hard, for sure, but God does not pour out his grace so we can keep it for ourselves; it is for our city. We put money behind Inhabit. We put staff behind Inhabit. We put energy behind Inhabit.

In the summer of 2012, Bank of America donated an old, foreclosed, boarded-up home in the central city to Inhabit. So for the next six months, we used the people resources of the church to completely rehab this house. It was a ton of work, but we believe it was all worth it. It has cost a lot of money, but we believe that the money is not ours anyway. Four women from our church were called to live in the home—all of them work other jobs but want to be part of something bigger than themselves. So we trained and commissioned them, and now they are living in this house in the middle of the city.

Their first assignment is to listen. For the whole first year, listen to the neighbors. Don't teach anything; just learn. Don't give anything; just receive. So that's what they are doing, living, learning, listening, taking, and becoming part of the neighborhood.

It's a beautiful sight. Four women taking on the call to become missionaries to their neighbors. Living out the way of Jesus in radical and culture-defying ways. They are living in a big story and have amazing stories to tell.

This is becoming who we are. A little faithfulness goes a long way. In the coming years, we will have many more people from our church living intentionally in under-resourced communities.

We will have many more of our people working on broken-down homes to bring transformation to neighborhoods. We will see more and more kids come into contact with loving and generous followers of the resurrected Jesus.[2]

I'm sure we will have more people living in these homes get robbed. I'm sure others will have their cars stolen or their stuff vandalized. It goes with the territory. We also prepare ourselves for something worse. The people living in these homes are covered in prayer. They are, in every way, modern-day urban missionaries.

Is it dangerous? Maybe. Is it risky? Yes. But we think it is more dangerous to miss out on what God is doing. It is more dangerous to think only of ourselves. It's more dangerous to use God's grace and blessing on ourselves. We do that long enough, and we too may try to throw Jesus off a cliff when he speaks truth to us. Choosing this life is hard and will cost us something. Choosing to create and support this ministry is hard and costs our church much. But we must continue to choose to reach the outsiders so they will not be outsiders any longer. We must continue to choose to partner with God as he brings the year of the Lord. Because if you aren't for him, you are indeed against him.

What good can come from the dangerous, broken city? Well, what good could come from Nazareth? Maybe the places that seem the most unlikely are exactly the places that God is working to bring new life. My advice to you is to think about the most unlikeliest place you think God would be and go there.

5

RIDING GIANTS

Have you ever heard of Laird Hamilton? He's a surfer and apparently a pretty important one. I hadn't heard of him either. Remember, I grew up in the mountains, not on the beaches of Southern California. I can tell you the history of moonshining, but not surfing.

That changed one day when I saw a documentary about Laird Hamilton on TV.[1] Up until this point in my life, I hadn't cared about surfing. But after this documentary, I was totally hooked.

The film is about Laird Hamilton attempting to surf the biggest wave that had ever been surfed. A monster wave nearly seventy feet tall off the coast of Tahiti in a place called Teahupo'o (pronounced CHO-PO). Teahupo'o's legendary reputation for wave riding is partly due to its unique form. An extremely shallow coral reef, which ranges up to twenty inches beneath the water's surface, is responsible for a very hollow-breaking wave. Whatever all that means. What we know is that people die on these waves. Only a handful in the world can surf them.

What is remarkable about Laird's accomplishment is not that he rode the wave, but *how* he rode the wave. Riding a wave like this had never been done before. There was no manual, no example for how to do it. It was going to take creativity. It was going to take imagination.

First, the wave was offshore, so his first problem was simply getting to the wave. Then Laird was faced with a second challenge: the wave was so big and traveling at such a high speed that the standard method of paddling into the wave was not going to work. He would need more speed to catch up to the wave.

Laird's companions initially tried to tow him into the wave, using a tow rope from a small boat. Quickly they realized this would not work; to get Laird into the right position would risk the *boat* being caught and crushed in the wave. And Laird was going to ride this wave. After a few hours, they changed plans and began using a jet-ski to tow him in.

Now you will have to excuse my lack of knowledge about surfing here, but apparently the standard boards of the day were not suitable to ride this massive and fast wave. So Laird designed a new type of board. A smaller, faster board that would provide both the stability and speed he needed to ride this monster.

Remember, this had never been done before. But Laird knew it could be done, and he was not going to be limited by the lack of existing resources. If needed, he would imagine new ways of looking at the world, of riding these huge waves.

As the documentary moves forward to the ride itself; it puts you right there. Laird is being towed into the wave on the Jet

Ski. The pilot of the Jet Ski, Darrick Doerner, recalls the moment he was towing Laird in: "I towed him onto this wave and it was to the point where I almost said, 'Don't let go of the rope,' and when I looked back he was gone."[2]

In a matter of seconds, the ride was over. Laird did it. He surfed this giant. A picture of Laird on the wave landed on the cover of the August 2000 issue of *Surfer* magazine. The wave became known as the "heaviest ever ridden."

One commentator in the film says, "Laird's wave at Teahupo'o was the most amazing, single most significant ride in surfing history, more than any other ride. Because what it did completely restructured collectively our entire perception of what was possible . . . normally, surfers are dragging their left hand on the face, but Laird had to drag his right hand, his back hand, on the opposite side of his board to keep himself from getting sucked up in that hydraulic. You know, in the middle of that maelstrom, how did his mind say, 'This is what I have to do?' No one had ever ridden as Laird rode on that wave before, and so it was the imagination of dealing with that unimaginable energy and coming up with the plan spontaneously. He couldn't practice."[3]

That might be one of the most significant statements I have ever heard: "The imagination of dealing with that unimaginable energy and coming up with the plan spontaneously." I love that.

PROPHETIC IMAGINATION

Laird was a dreamer. He did not see what was impossible; he saw what was possible. Prophets are dreamers too. They don't see the world as we see it; they see the world as it should be.

But in order to see the world as it should be, one has to see clearly the world that is. This is not optimism. Giant waves are not ridden with optimism; they are ridden by seeing the unimaginable problem and then creatively solving that problem. They realize that there is simply no way we can engage this problem with the tools we have on hand. We must create new tools and new methods. This takes vision.

Prophets have this vision, this imagination. Prophets see the way the world is more clearly than you or I, and they have the God-inspired vision to lead others to engage the world. You and I may see a bad school system, but the prophets see systemic injustice. You and I see porn as sin, but the prophets see it as the economic force that sustains a multibillion-dollar sex industry that profits off the slavery and rape of innocent victims. To the prophets, any human-diminishing activity is an assault on God's precious humanity.

In his classic commentary *The Prophets*, the great Jewish rabbi Abraham Joshua Heschel says, "To us a single act of injustice—cheating in business, exploitation of the poor—is slight; to the prophets, a disaster. To us injustice is injurious to the welfare of the people; to the prophets it is a deathblow to existence: to us, an episode; to them, a catastrophe, a threat to the world. . . . To the prophets even a minor injustice assumes cosmic proportions."[4]

The prophets understand that one injustice can wreck God's good creation, and they refuse to ignore even the smallest problems. They see the world as it should be. They always have before them the vision of redemption, the imagination of recreation.

Where are our prophets today? Where are our dreamers for this time? Where are those who see past the way the world looks to the way the world should look? Where are those who demand justice for the smallest offense against God's humanity?

Walter Brueggemann has a lot to say about prophets in his writing. He writes about imagination in his book *The Prophetic Imagination*: "We need to ask not whether it is realistic or practical or viable but whether it is *imaginable*. We need to ask if our consciousness and imagination have been so assaulted and co-opted by the royal consciousness that we have been robbed of the courage or power to think an alternative thought."[5]

It seems that as a church, we are losing our ability to dream, to imagine a new world. We have become so accustomed to this world, to the way things are done here, so assaulted by the consciousness of the culture around us, the "royal consciousness," that we have trouble thinking an alternative thought. We are losing our ability to dream, to look at the world around us and see newness as a possibility.

When was the last time you had an alternative thought? Not a thought that you've heard before, but a new one. When we are faced with a problem, we typically search online or in a book for help. We fall into the patterns of what others have done. We have one dreamer and a thousand implementers. We think that if we can just do this or that or whatever the latest church growth strategy is, our church will grow. If we can just get a youth pastor. If we can just start a new service. If we can just get some new music.

Can we not dream of a new world anymore? Have we become so pragmatic, so devoid of creativity that we can't face challenges with new ideas?

Do you have dreamers around you? Those who are constantly coming up with new ideas? How many artists do you have in your life? Artists look at the world and see something else, something that is not there. They look at a blank canvas and see what that canvas could potentially hold.

If we are going to be people of risk, we are going to need some prophets, dreamers, and artists to paint new worlds for us, new possibilities. Why? Because the royal consciousness—the consciousness of our culture—desires to keep us locked in the cage of the status quo.

The prophets were able to see a new world because they had so deeply immersed themselves in God's story that they knew nothing was impossible and nothing was improbable. They painted a picture that no one else was painting, a picture of destruction and then redemption. The cultural consciousness always tells us everything will be OK. Just keep doing what you're doing and things will work out. Keep the status quo. The royal consciousness denies grief, recreation, and imagination because all these threaten their hold on the minds of those they wish to rule.

Well, as the prophets so vividly show us, the royal consciousness is often wrong. Things don't always go right. Families fall apart. Neighborhoods get boarded up. Churches close. Kids shoot each other with guns. Status quo leaves slaves enslaved. Status quo leaves the broken broken.

To see redemption, we must always see the world through the prophetic imagination. Not dreaming of a fairy-tale land, but rather seeing the world as moving toward God's newness of redemption.

This is why the book of Revelation is so dangerous. Today it seems the church has reduced the book of Revelation to a timeline, to a manual for surviving the Apocalypse, instead of what it really is—the lens to see the world as God sees it. The book of Revelation was written to an oppressed people who were suffering and giving their lives for Christ, people who were being dominated by the Romans. It was proclaiming to them, "Christ is King over all creation. Caesar is not Lord. Jesus is, and he is bringing his redemption to this world—a new world is coming! Hold on! God is bringing newness!" Revelation supercharges our imagination for seeing past the death and despair all around us to see the work that God is doing behind the scenes to bring about a whole new world, a whole new system, a whole new . . . new.

Caesar doesn't want us to see that world because *that* world gives us hope. It gives us something to believe in. It reorients our imagination. It revolutionizes our expectation.

The lie of the royal/cultural consciousness is to keep our focus on the self-centered present. Focus on yourself. Newness is not really possible, so why worry about it? Just worry about yourself. We have become managers who believe there are no real mysteries to honor, only problems to be solved. We have become blind optimists who believe God has no business other than to maintain our standard of living. We have cut off our neighbors from our lives, believing that we can make our own future without the help of others.

Brueggemann agrees: "The royal consciousness with its program of achievable satiation has redefined our notions of humanness, and it has done that to all of us. It has created a subjective consciousness concerned only with self-satisfaction. It has denied the legitimacy of tradition that requires us to remember, of authority that expects us to answer, and of community that calls us to care. It has so enthroned the present that a promised future, delayed but certain, is unthinkable."[6]

We have been lulled to sleep by self-satisfaction. Our dreams have been stolen, because all we can see is ourselves. We can't even see God any longer. We have become numb to the creative and new ways God can and will work in us and through us, and because of this, we are unwilling to embark upon any new adventures. We have come to think there are no new possibilities, and so we are left with no new stories. "We do not believe that there will be newness but only that there will be merely a moving of the pieces into new patterns."[7]

We go to clean house, to declutter, but we feel so attached to our stuff that we simply rearrange. Our churches are suffering, so we change worship styles. We are just moving the pieces into new patterns. Our lives feel empty, so we get a new job or move to a new city. What we need is fundamental newness, recreation, transformation.

What's wrong is our lack of vision, our lack of ability to see the possibility of anything new. But imagining a new world is risky. Seeing God's dreams instead of our dreams is dangerous. It will cost us something. Just ask the prophets.

STAYING

When I was in seminary, we talked about our ultra-mobile culture and how the church needs to adjust to meet the needs of individuals who will only be in our churches for three to five years.

This makes sense, right? People move on average every three to five years. People move for a new job, move because they graduate from college, move to get married, move when they get divorced. We "take a better opportunity" or "want a fresh start."

This is nice for the people moving, but it is hard for those left behind, those who either choose not to move or simply cannot move. This trend is common in the church as well, as pastors from all varieties choose to leave the church they are in to move on to a better opportunity. Bigger congregations, more money, more opportunities. It's often easier to move and get a fresh start than to wade through difficult times together.

I realize that moving is a part of life. Many times there are good reasons to move. Sometimes we are called to move. Moving to a new place is not evil. I tell people as they consider moving to ask themselves this question: Am I moving to make my life better, easier and more efficient, or am I moving to serve God in a greater way?

Every move in Scripture—every single one—is people moving for the purpose of serving God, not serving themselves. Most of those moves headed into harder situations, situations that required more trust, faith, and endurance, not easier ones that enhanced their self-satisfaction.

For us Americans, it is hard to stay in one place. It is risky to be so involved in a single place that staying means sacrificing career opportunities, battling through seasons of sorrow and strife. Maybe the riskiest element of all is investing yourself so deeply with your neighbors and friends, your church community, and your mission that you simply cannot bear the thought of leaving.

Many of us often say, "I will really get involved and serve the church when I'm in a place that I can get settled in." Really? What version of God's story is this in? The problem with this is that we move to a place and realize that this place is not exactly the place we thought it would be, so we begin our exit strategy early on and begin to look ahead to the next place.

Then we move and do it again. And the cycle continues. We are making decisions based on our self-satisfaction, and we are finding ourselves increasingly less satisfied. We wait and wait until we get to where we want to be, but the problem is that if we finally get to where we want to be, we've missed half of our lives.

We live like zombies, roaming the land as dead shells of ourselves looking for something to devour. Our culture is fascinated with zombies these days. Maybe this is because we are living like zombies. No passion. No commitment. Just self-satisfaction.

The prophets have much to say about our ultra-mobile, zombie-like, disengaged, safety-driven culture that seems to only care for ourselves and would quickly leave our neighbor in pursuit of personal advancement.

People don't like the prophets because they point out to us the very things we do not want to deal with, the inner struggles of our humanity in relationship to God that we would rather leave hidden. The prophets demand more from us because they see what the world can be, not the world that is. They see our lives for what they could be, not necessarily what they are.

Take Jeremiah for example. Nice kid. Everybody liked him until he started telling them stuff they didn't want to hear. Then things changed.

Here's the situation: The people of Israel had been living in Babylon for generations. They had been living in exile, away from their homeland, and they wanted to return. They really wanted to go home. Then over the years, preachers rose up and began to preach messages of comfort and joy to the people. They were saying things like, "People of Israel! Your deliverance has come, God has heard your cry and you are going home. Pack your bags, because you are getting out of this foreign land. Get ready to go home. God is going to bless you and advance your careers."

The people liked this message. They packed their bags. They were ready to move. But Jeremiah had a different message. Jeremiah said, "Wait, everybody. Settle down! God has indeed heard your cry, but you are not getting out of exile yet. You have a ways to go. You are here for a lot longer." And then he went on to say:

> This is what the LORD Almighty, the God of Israel, says to all those I carried into exile from Jerusalem to Babylon: "Build houses and settle down; plant gardens and eat what they produce. Marry and have sons and daughters; find wives for your sons and give your daughters in marriage, so that they too may have sons and daughters. Increase in number there; do not decrease. Also, seek the peace and prosperity of the city to which I have carried you into exile. Pray to the LORD for it, because if it prospers, you too will prosper." (Jer. 29:4–7)

Unpack your bags. Build houses and settle down. Plant gardens. Marry. You are going to be here a while, so settle down, make a home, make a future—in exile. Make a future in the land you don't like. Make a home in the place you don't really want to be. Seek prosperity in the place your career is floundering and be part of the city that you might not even like right now.

But Lord, we don't like it here! The schools aren't that great. The food here is all wrong. The people here don't talk like us; they don't see the world like us. Oh Lord, you must be mistaken. This could not be the place you want us to stay.

This could not be what God wants. But remember. Life is not about you; it's about God.

A few verses later, we find the most famous line of Jeremiah that our Christian culture likes to quote: "'For I know the plans I have for you,' declares the LORD, 'plans to prosper you and not to harm you, plans to give you hope and a future'" (Jer. 29:11). When people quote this verse I doubt they realize that God is saying, "I know what I'm doing. Trust me. You want to get out of this mess, but I'm keeping you in it. So stay there and build a home in the mess. I've got a plan for you, but I also have a plan for the outsiders, and this is where it starts."

Seek the prosperity of the city. Seek its benefit. Not yours, but the city's. For the city to prosper, it needs you. For the city to be blessed, it needs you there. If you move out, it doesn't have a chance. So stay. Be part of something bigger than yourself and your pursuit of self-satisfaction. Be a restorer.

RESTORERS

In his book *The Next Christians*, Gabe Lyons lays out a case that the next movement of Christians will not have a theology of escapism or withdrawal, but rather they will see themselves as God's agents of restoration.[8] That restoration will be our defining feature.

Lyons and Q: Ideas for the Common Good[9] have done much to begin the process of moving the church out of culture wars to seeing our role as restorers of broken streets.

The truth is, the church lost the culture war. The church has lost its place of prominence in our culture today in the West. This is actually a good thing. We have for too long been spending too much of our time and energy on fighting scientists or fighting the courts to defend our ideological positions. These things are sometimes needed, but not to the level that we staked our whole identity on these battles. I'm glad we have lost our prominence and power in society. Maybe now we will begin to focus on people instead of our ideological positions. Christianity has always suffered when we have had prestige and power within a society. We are at our best when we are marginalized, pushed to the brink, persecuted, and given little power or privilege within a society. Then, and only then, do we have to rely fully on the power of God's story, on the power of God's Spirit.

His story and Spirit are about the restoration of the world and all that is within it. (See Rev. 21–22.) God doesn't need to be defended; the widow does. God can defend himself; the orphan cannot.

This is certainly not the first time that God's people have found themselves losing sight of their mission, blinded by their power and prosperity. Power and prosperity usually lead us to bad places. It takes all we are to seek humility and simplicity, generosity and compassion. Jesus had no power and no prosperity.

Following Jesus will cost us these things, but they will not initially be taken away by force. We are called, rather, to willingly give them away. But if we do indeed refuse to pursue the path of downward mobility, then God, in our best interest, may forcibly remove power and prosperity.

This is what was happening when the prophet Isaiah spoke to the people of Israel. The people had lost sight of their God-given mission and identity. They began to worship their blessing instead of worshiping the Blesser. They began to forget those they were called to protect and defend. They began to hoard the grace God had poured out on them, instead of willingly giving it away. So the prophet Isaiah stepped in and lashed the people. He told them God hated their false worship and selfish fasting, that they were neglecting the poor among them, and that God didn't care about their songs or liturgies if they were neglecting the very heart of living for God (see Isa. 58).

We must remember that even though the prophets may be hard on us, they always end with hope, because they see what we cannot see; they see the way the world should be. They have the divinely inspired prophetic imagination to see what the canvas is capable of looking like. The prophet sends out a message of remembrance to the people. He tells them what is possible. He declares to them their calling, their God-given destiny as a people. They were not called to spend their blessing on themselves. They were not called to live in safety or isolation. They were called to spend themselves on behalf of the poor, the oppressed, and the marginalized, and to restore the broken streets and broken systems. They were called to be restorers.

Isaiah declared:

> If you do away with the yoke of oppression, with the pointing finger and malicious talk, and if you spend yourselves in behalf of the hungry and satisfy the needs of the oppressed, then your light will rise in the darkness, and your night will become like the noonday. The LORD will guide you always; he will satisfy your needs in a sun-scorched land and will strengthen your frame. You will be like a well-watered garden, like a spring whose waters never fail. Your people will rebuild the ancient ruins and will raise up the age-old foundations; you will be called Repairer of Broken Walls, Restorer of Streets with Dwellings. (Isa. 58:9–12)

If you live like you are called to live—living out this extravagant life of following Jesus—then you will live into your God-given destiny to be the ones to rebuild the ancient ruins, to repair the broken walls, to restore the streets of dwelling.

We, like those before us, are called to be restorers. It is a big calling that can change the world. But being a restorer is risky; it's dangerous to our systems of self-satisfaction. We will have to sacrifice what we have and who we are to bring life to those around us. We will have to reorient our structures of time and movement. We will have to get dirty. Restoration will cost us something.

But this is our calling, our mission, our God-given destiny and purpose! We are called to partner with God in the restoration of the world, the restoration of people's spiritual lives, the restoration of people's physical lives, the restoration of our cities and neighborhoods. Our calling is no less than total and complete restoration, partnering with God and empowered by the Spirit to restore the world.

In order to restore the world, we will have to invest ourselves in the world. In order to restore our cities and the lives around us, we will have to invest, we will have to dwell, we will have to seek the prosperity of the places and people around us. Our motivation needs to be the prophetic motivation, the motivation to see how the world ought to be, not how it is. To see the world as it ought to be instead of how it is will take a lot of imagination and creativity. We must see past the white, naked canvas to see what the canvas is capable of holding. We must see past the labels of "poor" or "broken" or "addicted" to see the image of God in all people.

Just because the wave has never been surfed does not mean the wave cannot be surfed. We must see new possibilities, new angles, new ways of doing things. We cannot simply move the pieces around; we must create new pieces, new scenarios. We might need to create a new board or a new way of getting pulled into the wave. We might even have to spontaneously change the way things are done. To drag our back hand.

Church, we are being called to ride giants, to engage in the systematic issues of injustice and oppression that seem impossible to change. The giants of injustice hold people down, they dictate the course of lives, and they enslave people all around us. As God's people, we are called to engage them, to creatively unleash the power of the Spirit in and around brokenness.

We see this most vividly in our culture in our cities. Our cities are full of injustice and oppression. These oppressive forces seem to gather in our cities, and the rest of our culture looks at our cities and sees nothing but brokenness. So we stay away. We become afraid to go in. We believe there is no hope there. The people have a different political ideology, so we think they are lost forever. All we see is what the royal consciousness wants us to see. All we think is what Pharaoh wants us to think.

But we must remember this: nothing is unredeemable. Nothing is beyond transformation. Pharaoh is wrong! The oppressed and marginalized residents of our cities bear the image of God. They've been branded at creation with the mark of the God of creation. Let us look past our fears and prejudices and see that our cities are not ugly and dangerous. Rather, they are beautiful and holy, and God wants to redeem every part of them—every alley, every home, every life. Our cities hold the blessings of God, not the curse of our society!

This will be hard; it will be dangerous. We might just lose something. We might have to reimagine urban ministry. We might have to reimagine what the church looks like in our cities. We might need to create new ways for people to invest, new funding structures, new standards of success, new ways to tell our stories. We might need new ways to get towed into the wave and new boards to ride on.

Pharaoh doesn't want to give up his slaves. Caesar doesn't want to lose his power. Injustice will not go quietly.

But we are God's people, carrying the power of his Spirit with a God-given destiny to restoration. So let us be restorers. Let us engage. Let us stay. Let us pursue downward mobility for the sake of the hurting and hopeless. Let us get on our boards and ride new waves. Seeing not what is impossible or improbable, but rather seeing what is possible through the lens of our prophetic and divine imagination. Let us use the prophetic imagination to deal with that unimaginable energy of injustice and oppression in our cities and come up with the plan spontaneously to ride these giants!

PLACE OF THE SKULLS

The story of Laird Hamilton inspires me. It tells us a different story, a story of what is possible if we believe—nothing short of miracles. But it also tells us that riding these giants is dangerous; and one thing is for sure: We must not be motivated by fear, but by faith that the God of all creation is working over and within history.

Remember the name of the wave Laird surfed? Teahupo'o. This word is literally translated in the native language as "place of the skulls."

Jesus faced his giant wave that was called the Place of the Skull as well. He saw the world through the lens of the prophet, seeing what was possible. He did not see a wooden cross. He did not see the place of curse. He saw life, resurrection, hope, and newness.

I hope we can see these things as well. I hope we can live into our God-given destiny to be restorers of what is to come. We might just find our place of the skull as well. But take heart. The only way for resurrection to spring up is for us to take the risk of death. Jesus said, "Truly I tell you, unless a kernel of wheat falls to the ground and dies, it remains only a single seed. But if it dies, it produces many seeds" (John 12:24).

6

FORECLOSED

This is a chapter about numbers. Big numbers. The first number is eight thousand. That's approximately the number of foreclosed homes in our city.[1]

The subprime housing bubble that burst in 2008 left our city in shambles. As you move through our city neighborhoods, you see house after house that has been foreclosed, abandoned, and boarded up. The city uses pieces of green four feet by eight feet ply board to board up doors and windows of these homes, hence the word *board-ups* to describe these houses. As you drive down the streets, green boards litter the landscape. Many of the homes become havens for squatters and drug dealers or makeshift brothels. When a home is foreclosed, it begins to drag down a neighborhood. One or two is manageable, but when every other house is foreclosed, boarded up, and abandoned, this creates a haven for crime and chaos. Our neighborhoods were being foreclosed, boarded up, and left for dead and moving from order to chaos.

That's the wrong direction.

Genesis tells us that in the beginning the earth was formless and void. The Hebrew writers were telling us that the world was in chaos. Contrary to popular opinion, the central component of the creation narrative is not what happened on what day or analyzing how long a day actually was. The central component of the creation narrative is the creative force of God to move the world from chaos to order. Darkness to light. Terror to hope.

I was watching the science channel one night with my son, and some physicists were telling us that the natural progression of the universe is that of moving toward chaos—phenomena that destroy and bring chaos, such as black holes, supernovas, asteroids, gamma rays, rogue planets, and apparently the most terrifying of them all, star bursts.

The universe is moving toward chaos . . . and so are we. We see this all around us: Families fall apart; drugs ravage a community; economic and racial oppression separate and isolate; somebody takes a gun into a school and opens fire.

We live in a world of death, and death is always violent. It's obvious. Genesis 1 reminds us that our God is not a God of chaos but a God of order. God moves from chaos to order. God takes nothing—darkness and death—and makes something new and beautiful. We are ambassadors, agents, of this God-movement to order.

Foreclosures and green boards are a move to chaos.

My mentor, Dr. Jo Anne Lyon, often asks me, "If your church didn't exist, would the city miss it?" That's a good question. I don't have an answer to that question yet, but we are working on it. I don't know if our city would miss us yet, but that question keeps us up at night.

I heard Rick Warren say once, "You overestimate what you can do in five years and underestimate what you can do in twenty years." This is true. We often come out of the gate with such passion and force that we think we can systematically change the direction of the earth's spin in three years. I thought this too. But moving from chaos to order takes time. Chaos burrows itself in . . . deep. Building the foundation of restoration takes time, so what is really required is longevity . . . staying the course—time and pressure.

We can only take so much chaos before we have to make a decision. Either it will change us, or we will change it. Eight thousand foreclosed homes is too many. We became angry. Angry that our neighborhoods were being foreclosed and nobody was doing anything about it. Angry that the same neighborhoods that once had children playing ball in the streets were now full of chaos.

Whose fault was this? Somebody must be to blame, right? There are many moving parts to this chaos: a bad economy, the loss of jobs, under-resourced neighborhoods, and so on. There were many factors. But as we investigated this further, we saw one common thread to the plight of our neighborhoods: the banks.

The banks that owned these properties had made a lot of bad loans over the past few years. Loans that were terribly risky and depended upon a very high-functioning economy. These loans that had been made with fine print and given to anyone who had a signature a few years earlier were now set to balloon with interest. Everyone had jumped on the bandwagon of home ownership—people who could not really afford a home, landlords who wanted to make a quick buck—and now everything was crashing down.

Many communities felt the weight of this millstone falling from the sky, but cities felt it in a unique way. Cities created the perfect storm of foreclosure. Poverty plus bad loans plus job loss, combined with density, equals disaster. No one saw this coming. How could they? Everyone seemed to be blinded by their greed. The big banks that had made these loans and now owned these foreclosed homes were letting the results of their bad bets just sit and rot . . . and pull down our neighborhoods with them. The real question to us was this: Does anyone really care? These were neighborhoods in the city, in economically poor zip codes. Did they really matter? Did they really count?

When a tree falls in the forest, does anyone hear it? When eight thousand homes are left abandoned in a small geographic area, does it matter? Yes, it does.

JUBILEE

A person once asked me, "What does redemption look like in the city?" This is an interesting question, isn't it? Think about it. Why would anyone even ask it like this and include the phrase "in the city"? Why would redemption look any different in the city than it does anywhere else?

But it is different, albeit slightly. The short answer to this question is this: jubilee.

For most of us, much of the time, redemption is about the personal renewal we find as we surrender our lives to Jesus. It is about being saved from our sin and being made right in relationship to God. Redemption is about leaving our exile and embarking upon a personal relationship with the God and King of creation: Jesus Christ. It changes everything for us—changes the way we see the world, the way we treat others, the way we live, and the way we think.

This idea of personal salvation, personal redemption, is a central component of the message of Scripture—that we can have a personal relationship with God now and forever. Our eyes can be opened. We can be set free. We can be made new.

This links us back to the mission of Jesus in Luke 4:18–19. Jesus was coming to bring redemption to both the personal and to the systematic.

You see, jubilee is about the system, and the systems must be redeemed and made whole. The Year of Jubilee was a systematic release of debts every fifty years. So if you had debts built up that were oppressing you and your family so that you simply could not move because of this crushing weight upon you, when the fiftieth year came, they would be removed. The Year of Jubilee was a system to limit long-term systematic oppression of any person or group of people. It was hope built into the system of life.

Systems matter. Systematic poverty is soul destroying because there is almost no way out of it. Systematic poverty creates schools that are underfunded and neglected and thus fail to inspire children to learn and achieve. Systematic poverty creates a lack of jobs that offer people that holy occupation of work to create self-dignity in themselves and their families and afford them the opportunity to provide for their loved ones. Systematic poverty forces people to fend for themselves and creates a dog-eat-dog world for pure survival. Systematic poverty creates walls of division between those who have and those who don't. And on and on it goes. It's systematic because it is built into the systems of our economics and laws. It's not just "something that happens." It's built up and sustained. It is policed.

These systems need redemption. Yes, we all need personal redemption, but if the systems are not redeemed, not made whole and restored, then people are still going to be starving and dying and killing one another for crumbs.

This is why Jubilee is necessary. Jubilee is systematic redemption to the broken systems and division. And Jubilee is most necessary in our cities because it is distinctly within the American city that we see the most systematic neglect and oppression. Jubilee destroys the status quo within the systems. It says, "Reset."

Rich people don't like Jubilee. Middle-class people don't like it either. This is why the gospel is such good news to the poor. It's why the rich want to throw Jesus off a cliff. So what does redemption look like in the city? It looks something like this: The blind, broken, and prisoners are finding freedom, hope, and salvation through personal relationship with the creator God.

And the systems, laws, policies, and dividing walls that have built up and are causing hopelessness and pain are being reset and renewed to bring life instead of death. This is redemption both on the personal and systematic levels.

Eight thousand foreclosed homes is a lot. This is not an isolated event, this doesn't "just happen," this is not just a "coincidence." This is a systematic problem.

Our kids couldn't play in the street because of the drug deals that were happening on the corner. Moms were scared to live in their own homes because they felt like prisoners held for ransom.

Something had to change. The system needed to be reset.

After we investigated this issue for some time, we saw one common denominator—the banks. The banks were creating this system, and they were the only ones that could change the direction of this disaster. But how could anything change? The banks hold all the power. You can't take on a major international bank and live to tell about it. This is what the royal consciousness would like you to believe: "You can't do anything, so just forget about it. You take on these guys, and your life will be covered in green ply board." Keep the status quo.

Remember Laird Hamilton? Just because nobody has done it doesn't mean it's not possible. We will just have to reimagine new ways of bringing restoration to our neighborhoods. We might have to drag our back hand.

Sure, we couldn't take on a bank, but we could take on five.

COMMON GROUND

I was the last one to speak. There were five hundred of us gathered at Marquette University to kick off our "Foreclosure Campaign." I was the one responsible for sending us out, but this send-out was no regular send-out; we needed inspiration. You see, the fight ahead of us would be long and hard. It would take time and pressure. We could not rely upon a steady drip of the faucet that would only annoy our opponent. What we needed was a steady spray from a fire hose. We had to open the full pressure of the prophetic imagination.

At the end of my speech, I told the story of Moses going before Pharaoh and demanding that Pharaoh let God's people go. I told the crowd that we must stand before these banks and boldly declare, "Let our neighborhoods go free!" Everyone was excited. Then we went back to our homes on that cold Wisconsin night. None of us realized the fight that lay before us.

You see, our church is a part of a community organizing group called Common Ground.[2] Common Ground is a group of over fifty churches, a few synagogues, and a handful of small businesses that have come together to take on the pressing issues of injustice facing our city. Common Ground works mainly in the political arena, working with and sometimes against politicians to bring change through the systems of politics and business. Common Ground uses organized people to form organized power to take on these giants.

Alone we are weak, but together we are strong. To take on five major banks and demand that they give us our neighborhoods back, we had to stand together. We could not do this alone.

Our city was suffering, and as was discussed in the last chapter, we are called to seek the benefit of the city. We could see no better way to bless our city than this.

Now, let's be real here for a moment. Politics and church don't mix well. We seem to have trouble keeping the proper balances when we enter the realm of politics. We either refuse to enter this arena at all, or when we enter the arena we get sucked in and leave telling jokes and having cocktails with the mayor. Both of these approaches lack balance; they are both flawed. Refusing to engage is not the proper response, but neither is getting in bed with a political party. There is a delicate balance to walk here.

Common Ground is made up primarily of mainline churches (Catholics, Lutherans, Episcopalians) and African-American churches. It's a strange place for an evangelical, predominately young, white church (that's us) to find itself, but we are trying to take Jeremiah seriously. Trying to hear the cry of the city, and this is how the Spirit is leading.

Common Ground is giving us this opportunity to bless our city, to seek its benefit, and to see it prosper, so we joined them in their struggle. Our relationship with Common Ground has not always been easy. Many times we have not agreed with the organization on their stance or approach to situations. Sometimes their ideas of power do not line up with ours. We struggle with them, oftentimes disagreeing with one another about the approach to achieve our goals. Personally, I don't like power. No, strike that. I love power and want more of it, and that is why I must always remind myself that I don't like power, because I know what it can do to us. It can make us believe that we are something, that we can do things on our own, that people serve us. Satan continues to tempt us by saying, "See all this land? Just bow down and worship me and I will give you ultimate power. I will make you ruler."

It sounds good, but grasping for power will only lead to destruction. Rather, our calling is to take the position of the powerless, to always be giving any and every ounce of power we have away to those who are vulnerable and hurting. Power is given only to be given away, not ever to be kept. Power makes me uncomfortable because I'm drawn to it in such strong ways. When power is involved, we must always proceed with caution, always take self-inventories, always ask others to keep us accountable.

To be honest, this relationship with Common Ground is not the most strategic move toward church growth. We have lost people because of our relationship with them. We live in a very political world where people often gather around others that see the world in the same way they do. We often gravitate toward the ideas we like. Republicans group with Republicans and Democrats group with Democrats. Our church is split down the middle between Democrats and Republicans. This makes for difficult conversations sometimes. We have to remind ourselves that we are "in Christ" first and foremost. That we are brothers and sisters, no matter what our political affiliations are. This is hard sometimes, but if we value our brothers and sisters, then we will see and engage their position; we will wrestle with those positions. We may end up disagreeing on an issue, but that does not mean we cut off our relationship with one another. Politics will divide us if we let it, and the church is currently experiencing this all too clearly.

I believe, as John 17 lays out, the church is called to unity, and anything that divides us is not of Christ. We are called to unity—no matter what our political aspirations may be. We are first and foremost followers of Jesus—not Americans, not a political party, not our professions, but followers of Jesus.

So our relationship with Common Ground is risky for us. Sometimes when the group makes a move that we disagree with or do not agree with ideologically some people see that as us endorsing the move. This is a hard and delicate relationship. Maybe that's how politics should be entered. Always struggling, always a bit uncomfortable, always questioning and holding accountable.

Jesus was not apolitical, devoid of political engagement. Rather, he was always prophetic toward politics and its leaders, always holding politics to a standard of God's rule. This, too, is how we try to operate.

If we are going to embark upon the hard work of redeeming systems, then we must engage politics. Plain and simple.

Martin Luther King, Jr., a leader in the church-state journey said, "The church must be reminded that it is not the master or the servant of the state but rather the conscience of the state. It must be the guide and the critic of the state and never its tool. If the church does not recapture its prophetic zeal, it will become an irrelevant social club without moral or spiritual authority."[3]

For twelve long months, we had meeting after meeting with the banks. At first the banks laughed at us. We requested meetings with their CEOs and their regional representatives, but they refused to meet with us, so we started telling the stories of foreclosed neighborhoods and foreclosed lives to the media. They were compelling stories—stories that we all resonate with because they hit close to home. The media started picking it up, and pretty soon the banks were getting some pretty bad press in some major publications. They didn't like this, so they agreed to meet with us.

Mark Fraley, the lead organizer of Common Ground, told me once that our goal was to get a reaction from the banks, because when we get a reaction, we know we've hit a nerve. Our goal was to get a reaction. After months and months of work, we finally got it.

Our initial meetings with bank executives went nowhere. We were demanding that the banks take care of their properties. This included mowing the grass, scraping the snow, properly boarding up the properties, and maintaining them. They own them, and they should be responsible owners just like the rest of us.

They didn't like our tone.

We were also demanding that they knock down the houses they owned that were beyond repair. They told us this was the city's responsibility. Interesting, isn't it? They told us that we, the taxpayers, were responsible for tearing down the homes that they owned and left for dead. (It cost between ten thousand and fifteen thousand dollars to knock down each home.)

We didn't like their tone.

Then we demanded that each bank put up twenty million dollars apiece to form a rehab fund to restore these old foreclosures, fix them up, and then sell them to low-income individuals with responsible and fair mortgages.

That's where the meetings usually ended. So we would shake hands, smile, and open up the fire hose some more.

After repeated meetings with bank executives, slowly getting to higher and higher individuals, after trips to stockholder meetings in Germany and California, an amazing and unlikely force aligned with ours: the German media. Deutsche Bank, a German bank, was one of the worst offenders, and once the German public caught wind of this, they were outraged. On a side note, why weren't Americans outraged like the Germans at the activities of our banks? Adam Smith, the father of capitalism, said that businesses exist to serve the general welfare, and when a business fails to serve that general welfare, then they forfeit their right to exist.

Deutsche Bank has no US branches, so two of our leaders went to Germany, to the Deutsche Bank shareholder meeting and, after a long wait, stood before the CEO and told them what was happening in Milwaukee. They spoke in German and told the CEO, "German immigrants built Milwaukee, and now Germans are destroying Milwaukee." The German media pounced on this, doing a series of newspaper articles, creating a documentary, and putting our leaders on the German equivalent of *Sixty Minutes*.

The discussions began to change.

On October 24, 2010, one thousand members of Common Ground of Southeastern Wisconsin gathered in the Harley Davidson auditorium with representatives from five major multi-national banks.

I again had the honor of speaking to the crowd to outline our journey thus far and the demands we had made to these banks. I reminded the crowd of our gathering twelve months before when I had told them that God heard the cry of our city and we were going before Pharaoh (the banks) to demand that they let our neighborhoods go. I reminded them that God always hears the cry of the oppressed. I then asked each bank representative if they would agree to partner with us in the restoration of our city, if they would agree to the list of our demands to help restore our foreclosed neighborhoods. As I walked over and shook each one of their hands, they all agreed. Yes, they all agreed to take care of their properties, to knock down at their own expense homes that were beyond repair, and to fund the rehab efforts as well.

As a collective group, they committed to 33.8 million dollars in rehab and loans. Not quite what we wanted, but 33.8 million dollars was more than anyone on the outside ever thought we'd get.

Today, homes in under-resourced neighborhoods, formerly foreclosed and boarded-up homes, are being remodeled and sold to low-income families at affordable prices. Neighborhoods are being restored. Hope is being restored. Lives are being restored.

Our relationship with Common Ground is not always easy. We sometimes step on one another's toes. It costs us something, but at the end of the day, our city is being blessed and is prospering because of Common Ground's ability to organize. So we will continue to partner with them to bring restoration.

Currently, as I write this, we are beginning to engage our broken school system. Kids deserve to learn, and through our partnership with Common Ground, we will seek to make sure these kids can learn.

This is just one way our imagination is being cultivated. One house here; one house there. No more green ply board. That's hope.

Jesus said something about the kingdom of God looking a lot like a mustard seed. Starting small . . .

LITTLE GIRLS

Now we come to our second number: twenty-seven million. That's how many modern-day slaves there are in the world, most of these being girls caught up in the biggest business in the world: sex trafficking.

I was working on my house one day when I received a call from my friends at International Justice Mission (IJM).[4] Transformation City Church is part of DIVE, IJM's network of churches seeking justice. We support their work to eradicate modern slavery and defend the poor from other violent oppression. They were calling to see if we could help send postcards to our senator to get his support on an upcoming bill called the Child Protection Compact Act.

This bill would help fund the Trafficking in Persons Office within the US State Department. It would fund efforts, like the ones by IJM, to work with local officials to cut down on sex trafficking and underage prostitution in under-resourced countries. The passing of this bill would directly lead to the freedom of little girls from being sex slaves.

This bill was about systems.

I knew we could do better than simply send in some postcards. So over the course of the next three months, we organized churches from all across the state of Wisconsin. Then, on the same day at the same time, over one hundred people from all across the state showed up at three different offices of the senator, personally delivering over one hundred letters asking for his support of this important legislation. (We told him we were coming beforehand, of course.)

When we gathered outside the senator's downtown Milwaukee office, his assistant met us with a personal note from the senator telling us that because of our outpouring of support he would indeed support and cosponsor this bill. Our petitions turned into thanks.

As we worked more closely with IJM, we began to imagine and dream what this would look like on a local level. Was human trafficking and underage prostitution an issue for us in our city? We began to pray, to listen, to dream and imagine.

Through our year-long community assessment research, we found that underage prostitution is indeed an issue for us locally. We heard stories of fifteen-year-old girls offering sex for five dollars. Poverty, drugs, lack of jobs, and poor educational systems create systems that prey on teenage girls.

Maybe these girls believe the promise of a pimp who tells them they are beautiful. Maybe they've never heard from anyone else in their whole lives that they are beautiful, valuable, and wonderful. When they hear it for the first time from a pimp who is out to trick them, they jump into his car. Then the pimp drugs them up and sells them like cattle to his "friends." Maybe they were abused as children by their mom's boyfriend, a stepdad, a brother, or a cousin, and they feel they have nothing to lose by profiting from their sexual exploitation. So they begin to turn a few tricks to make some extra money, and then they get caught up in the underworld of underage prostitution. All because some predator decided to use his strength to force himself on a defenseless, beautiful little girl. (Note: Of course, not all predators are male.) Or sometimes it's a family member who pushes them out onto the street, or offers "private visits" to their daughter's room in exchange for cash or drugs or to pay the rent. Or it may be as simple as a teenager who genuinely fell in love, accidentally became pregnant, decided to keep her baby even when the father took off, and now she is out on her own trying to raise a child, finish school, and stay alive. Offering her body is the only possible way she sees to provide for her new baby whom she loves so much.

Whatever the reason, it is all around us.

I was recently talking to a woman who was a victim of sexual exploitation and is now working to help teenage girls get out of this life. She told me, "The only way not to see it is to not look." The church has been not looking for some time.

Sadly, most of us would rather not look, because if we don't see it, we can pretend it doesn't exist . . . so we can sleep at night. Maybe we need to sleep less. Maybe we need to stay awake at night with the heavy burden of these innocent lives being trashed by sexual evil.

This can't stand! This injustice has no place in the world God desires. This evil has no place in the kingdom and therefore no place on this earth either. So we as a church are dreaming; we are trying to imagine a new world on earth as it is in heaven.

Currently, we are working on pulling together a coalition of churches in our region to create an after-care facility, so the underage girls who want to get out of this life have a place to start.

I had another conversation with the Milwaukee police lieutenant who is in charge of the local trafficking and prostitution beat. She told me they couldn't give me a number of the known cases each year, but that there were many known cases each year of police picking up underage prostitutes. Some estimates are as high as 150. These girls are underage, so the police are required to treat them as victims of trafficking. I asked her what they do for those girls. The answer was astounding. She told me there's simply not much they can do for them. There is just nowhere safe for them to go. They are minors, so they cannot be held for prostitution, because technically they cannot be prostitutes since they are underage. The police are required by law to turn these girls back over to their legal guardians, who sometimes are the ones abusing them in the first place.

In June 2012, a joint effort between the FBI and local law enforcement collaborated with dozens of major cities to complete a synchronized raid called "Operation Cross Country." Shared Hope International posted a chart on the results of this raid and found that in every major city in the US, four to six girls were rescued as a result of this single raid on a single night. Milwaukee ranked as one of the highest with six girls rescued.[5] This is probably no different than your city. This problem is all over. We just choose not to look.

As we continued our research, a few things became apparent to us. The first is that these are not underage prostitutes; they are underage sex slaves. This is child rape. Second, we found that there was no long-term residential care for underage victims of sexual slavery and exploitation.

We as a church community are dreaming of a safe place for these little girls. A place of hope, a place of restoration. Our dreams are becoming a reality. In January 2013, after almost two years of research and community assessment, we formed a coalition of ten churches and launched "Exploit No More." The mission statement of this new organization is "to advance the kingdom of God through intentional efforts to end child sex slavery in the city of Milwaukee by awareness, advocacy, and long-term residential after care." Exploit No More is dedicated to empowering children to rise out of sexual slavery.[6] This organization will offer the first long-term residential recovery beds for underage victims of sexual exploitation in the state of Wisconsin.

We will not bury our heads in the sand and pretend this isn't happening in our city. This is injustice, and it needs to be confronted. This costs a lot of money and takes a lot of energy. It is dangerous to a church budget. This work is messy and sees very little "success." The laws need to be changed. Police forces need to be trained. Pimps don't like when their prized moneymakers are taken off the street, so they come looking for them.

The work of restoration is always risky business. It will always cost us something. Restoration never comes cheap. But we believe these little girls are worth it, that they are created in the image of God. Wouldn't you agree? They are someone's daughter, someone's future wife, someone's future mother. They are daughters of the King, and they are worth it. They have a future, a legacy to leave upon this earth.

These, among others you are reading about, are ways we are dreaming. Ways that we are imagining not what is, but what should be. Injustice is evil and does not have a place in God's kingdom. The church's calling is to come against injustice and evil in all of its forms. This sometimes puts us in places we are not comfortable with. This will cause us to struggle with others and ourselves. It is our calling.

Gabe Lyons says, "Along the way, church leaders have been demoted in the public consciousness as well. Once relied upon as key allies for discussions about city issues and public life, they have lost their place at the table. They rub shoulders with civic leaders in their communities with less frequency. And, unfortunately, many seem disinterested in investing in this relationship. Many churches are increasingly exhibiting less and less real influence in the communities where they're located. If they were gone tomorrow, one can't help wondering if anyone would notice."[7]

Would anyone notice if our church disappeared? I hope so. My dream is that if we disappeared the city would be affected. The only way to make that dream a reality is by investing, reaching, risking, and caring. To pour our lives out for the benefit of our city. To live, not for our own benefit, but for our city's.

These are big numbers, and the task is sometimes overwhelming. Oftentimes we look and feel as if we simply cannot do anything.

I will give you another number: one. It all starts with one. One life. Yours. Theirs. A journey begins with one step. The world is changed with one life.

7

MIKRONS

Facebook gives me anxiety. I don't use it much, but it draws me in for some reason. I'm a pretty private person, so I don't post what I'm doing or where I'm going or how many cheeseburgers I ate over the weekend. I think I liked the world a little better when we didn't know what everyone was doing all the time, because when I see what everyone is doing, for some reason I get anxious. I see that people are out having fun when I'm not. I see where friends are getting together, and I wasn't invited. I see where people from my church are off boating on the lake and ditched church. Or worse, I see where people who used to be in our church are now posting how great another church experience was for them. Facebook causes me to compare myself to other people. Is my life that fun? Is my church satisfying? Is our ministry the best?

Competition always breeds anxiety because competition is rooted in fear—fear of losing something, fear of not being good enough, fear of missing out on something. Competition breeds fear, fear breeds anxiety, and anxiety tells us that our life is not good enough.[1]

Anxiety is selling us a false story. Competition dictates to us which story we should value. Competition tells us that the story we need to be living in is the one where we are rich, save the planet from the villain, and get the girl in the end. If our lives are not living up to this, and we see that someone else's is, well then, we become anxious. We find ourselves living in the anxiety of a false story that says, "You are not good enough like you are; you need more. You need to be better, faster, stronger."

I find myself judging my life through the lens of others people's lives . . . competition. My church is not very big, and sometimes this causes me anxiety, so I miss what God is doing in and around me because I'm so focused on getting more so I can be living in the "better" story. Why is this?

A lot of it has to do with the stories we place value and emphasis on in our culture. In the church world, we value big churches. The bigger you are, the better you are. There's no middle ground here. We judge what God is doing in our churches by numbers—people and money. The more people you have, the more successful you are, plain and simple. The biggest churches are the best. The pastors of the biggest churches are the best. If you are not the biggest church, then you need to work harder to get to be the biggest.

We live in the story of the biggest—biggest house, biggest salary, biggest fan base, biggest retirement fund, and on and on. This is the story we hold up as the most valuable, the most important. The story we have begun to believe that God works the best through. If you aren't growing, then you are dying; and dying is not God's desire. (At least that's what the false story tells us.)

Recently I read a couple of articles on churches in the area on our local paper's website. One church was buying and remodeling an old vintage theater that seats a thousand.[2] Another was buying and remodeling an old Walmart.[3] Old Walmarts are pretty big. You must be a pretty impressive church if you are buying an old Walmart.

I admit I became a bit depressed. I was living in competition. I was valuing the story of bigger and more. I was "failing" because I wasn't remodeling a Walmart.

But aren't there other important stories besides bigger, faster, stronger? What about relocation? Does our culture have any place or value for the story of relocation?

I'm not talking about relocating to take a better job or so your kids can go to better schools. No, I'm talking about the intentional movement from one place to another for the kingdom. It has to be intentional because, left to our own desires, we always want to occupy the bigger, better, faster, stronger, richer story of upward mobility. It takes intentional energy, focus, and passion to give value to the story of downward mobility.

Relocation can look different for different people. The primary idea of relocation for our discussion is moving the place you call "home." Moving your primary residence from a place within a safe, luxurious, or comfortable neighborhood to a hurting, under-resourced, or not-so-comfortable neighborhood. Here's an example: Sell your home in the suburbs and move into the city. Moving from the comfortable into the difficult.

This movement always requires sacrifice, but if you look to the cloud of witnesses that have gone before us, you see that when God calls us to something, it is almost always a movement from comfort to sacrifice, from the story of upward mobility to the story of downward mobility. To make a decision to intentionally relocate your primary residence to benefit the hurting and oppressed, to move your life from being far away from pain and oppression to being very close, even living within this pain, to move your proximity—this story is not as popular. This story is not as dominant. I don't see people competing against one another to see who can relocate more people into under-resourced areas. I don't see newspaper articles about people selling their homes in the suburbs and moving into the cities. I don't see our church culture lifting up individuals who put their lives in danger to relocate.

But these stories are so much more compelling, don't you think? Everybody around us is after bigger, better, faster, and richer. Our world is filled with those stories of the pursuit of more. But the stories of sacrifice are the ones that give us chills, the ones that make us cry, the ones that shake us to the core. The stories of the pursuit of the one who is hurting and marginalized is the legacy of our faith, so why don't we emphasize these stories more? Does the church value kingdom virtues passed down to us from our Lord and King Jesus, or do we value American virtues more? Are we building a kingdom of comfort or a kingdom of sacrifice? Who are we actually following here: Jesus or the American dream?

FROM CUPBEARER TO WALL-REBUILDER

Nehemiah must have had a nice life. As cupbearer, he worked directly for the king. The king had to trust him implicitly, since Nehemiah was the last barrier between the king and the king's enemy. If someone got to Nehemiah, then they would have direct access to poisoning the king.

There must have been great benefits to this job. The king had to keep Nehemiah happy. The last thing a king wants is a disgruntled cupbearer, right? I can imagine that Nehemiah had a nice life: good house, great salary with government benefits, really good health and retirement benefits. His family must have been well taken care of. His status in the king's house would have been great. Besides, Nehemiah was a foreigner. What could have been a better job, especially for someone from another land?

But one day everything changed. His nice life was threatened. He heard the cry:

> In the month of Kislev in the twentieth year, while I was in the citadel of Susa, Hanani, one of my brothers, came from Judah with some other men, and I questioned them about the Jewish remnant that had survived the exile, and also about Jerusalem. They said to me, "Those who survived the exile and are back in the province are in great trouble and disgrace. The wall of Jerusalem is broken down, and its gates have been burned with fire." When I heard these things, I sat down and wept. For some days

> I mourned and fasted and prayed before the God of heaven. (Neh. 1:1–4)

God often breaks our hearts for the thing God wants us to engage in, the thing God wants us to give our lives to. Today, what breaks your heart? Nehemiah's heart was broken, not by a girl, but by the condition of his people. Nehemiah heard the cry. His heart was broken when he heard of the suffering of his people in Jerusalem, broken to hear that the wall of protection was broken down.

So Nehemiah did the natural thing any of us would do, right? He left his government job and relocated to the broken-down city of his ancestors. He changed his proximity to the pain. He went from far to near.

As we read the book of Nehemiah, it is hard to get a sense of the scope and difficulty of the work he did. We don't see the depth of opposition and danger he faced. The storyteller seems to assume that the reader knows a little about what a dire and hopeless situation it was and how hard the work would be to accomplish. To some extent, the difficulty in the story just seems insignificant. What mattered was that there were people hurting; the walls had been broken and restorers were needed.

All around our county, the walls of our cities have fallen, too. The systems of protection and care have deteriorated. They've been broken by invading injustices. The walls lie in rubble, and the people inside are suffering.

Reports of our cities spread. There is no lack of images that come from our newspapers, televisions, and magazines. Lives are falling to the invading armies of oppression and injustice. Teenage girls are being taken by the forces of evil to go serve the gods of our sexual appetites. There's no wall to protect them, so anyone can come in and do what they want. Our cities are unprotected.

But is anyone listening? Does this break your heart?

When you read that the people of our cities are starving, homeless, and jobless; that the school systems in our cities are deteriorating; that poverty is suffocating; that drugs are destroying and pimps are pimping—does this break your heart? Do you hear the cry? Do you mourn and fast? Or do you just turn the page? Change the channel? Do you respond in a way that we hear all too often: "Oh, those lazy people, they just need to get out and get a job." "They just need to invest in their kids." "They just all need to be thrown into jail."

Instead of broken hearts, we have hardened hearts. Pharaoh had a hardened heart. The Pharisees had hardened hearts. If we are not actively seeking to fix the walls, then we are probably destroying them. Ignoring the problem is being complicit with the problem. If we cannot hear the cry of the oppressed, then we are probably part of the system of oppression. Living with a hardened heart is bad news according to Scripture—really, really bad news.

The walls of our cities are broken, and the people are crying out for help. Will we hear? Or will we continue to live in our story of bigger?

Nehemiah could not repair the walls from Assyria. He couldn't engage the problems in the suburbs. He needed to relocate, to go live with the people. Some of you need to relocate.

TOM AND KELLY AND BRIAN AND BECKY

I remember when I first met Tom and Kelly. They came to visit our church at a rather inconvenient time for us. We had recently been kicked out of this very cool, hip theater that we were meeting in by the city of Milwaukee because of a zoning issue. But this left us in a bind. We had two weeks to find a new place to meet and were committed to staying in the geographic area we felt God calling us to.

We were in the process of purchasing and remodeling an old indoor archery range, but it would be months before it was ready to occupy. During this building project, we had to find another place to meet. It was more difficult than we anticipated because our time was limited and so few spaces were available for rent. We finally found a place, the only place. It was not very flattering, and that's being kind.

We were meeting in this old Christian Science Church that had been turned into an auction gallery. But we were not meeting in the sanctuary because it was too big for our size and had cats living behind the stage and animal droppings all over. The owners had not used the sanctuary in years and had let their two pet Shih-Tzus roam at will and had adopted some stray cats to keep in the back. It didn't smell good.

We had about one hundred people at the time, so we decided we could meet in the first-floor fellowship hall. It smelled weird and had no air conditioning, so it was really hot. There was no place for our nursery, so we asked parents to leave their babies in a makeshift room with a baby gate on one wall and a mobile divider on the other.

When people visited us, I was sure we'd never see them again. And sure enough, one Sunday, in walked Tom and Kelly with two young girls in tow and a third on the way. I was nice to them but thought, "We won't ever see these people again." They told me they lived completely on the other side of the city and were looking for another church.

They sat through my message, and after the service, I talked to them a bit. They said our church was exactly what they were looking for. They had been feeling very uncomfortable at their previous church and knew God was leading them to live out their faith in a greater way.

It quickly became apparent that Tom and Kelly were being called to relocate. They began the process of discernment and gathered as many people around them as possible and began to pray about their next steps. They pulled people in and became engaged in urban ministry. They began to walk and pray the streets of our city. They were beginning to believe. They put up their house for sale. They were going to move into an under-resourced neighborhood and live their lives poured out—pouring themselves out for the benefit of people around them. They were going to relocate.

It was not an easy decision for them to make. It was not a financially wise decision; they would be selling their home in a down market and buying a home in the city that they would have trouble ever reselling. People don't want to live in the city. We have more houses than we know what to do with. You can get a house for cheap, but you cannot view this purchase as a financial investment. Realistically, this was not their biggest concern. Their bigger concern was for their three beautiful young girls, all under the age of six.

Their family disapproved of their decision. Kelly came to me one day crying, feeling guilty that she was putting her daughters in danger. As we began to talk, she told me the reaction she was getting from her family and friends when she told them they were moving into the city. I was saddened by the perception some people had of the city. People told Kelly she was "endangering the lives of her girls." That they would be "shot or kidnapped or raped" if they moved there. That their kids would "have no chance at life after attending city schools." Kelly wondered, as any mother would, if she was putting her daughters' futures at risk.

This was the brutal reaction of her family to their decision. Sadly, this is the most common reaction to those who decide to relocate. Their closest friends and family often do everything in their power to persuade them not to move, because they see the city as a deathtrap.

But Tom and Kelly had broken hearts and were being called to repair broken walls.

As we talked, Kelly began to see God's heart once again instead of the division and segregated perceptions. My kids live in some of these same neighborhoods. They play outside; I don't worry. Other kids play in the streets; they survive.

It is simply amazing how the people living outside our city view people living inside our city. It is viewed as a jungle warzone. It breaks my heart. I am not from Milwaukee, and it breaks my heart to see and hear these perceptions. And this is all too common. I seriously hear these perceptions all the time. People ask me, "How can you live there?" and I live in a very quiet, racially mixed neighborhood.

Another couple, Brian and Becky, who made the choice to relocate from the suburbs tells me how hard it has been for them. Becky was on staff at a very big church in the suburbs, resigned, and moved to the city. They came to us because they felt God calling them to the city and wanted to be where people valued the city. They had broken hearts as well, but couldn't find anyone in their circle of friends who validated their call. They tell me often that the same people they were friends with while they were living in the suburbs are no longer friends with them. Those "friends" refuse to visit them at their home in the city. They honestly fear for their lives. They have cut off communication. This hurts. This causes doubt.

But because Brian and Becky made the choice to relocate, they are now in relationship with people they would never have had the chance to be in relationship with. Becky mentors one of the young girls living near our Community House. Her name is Jermesha; we call her Me-Me.

Me-Me is a precious young African-American girl in middle school who was having trouble in school. She really wanted to do well but was having a hard time. Becky noticed this and began talking to Me-Me about it. It turns out Me-Me could not see so well; she needed glasses. So Becky told the church, and the church connected Me-Me's family to an eye doctor. Together we were able to make sure Me-Me had glasses. Now she is doing great in school and loving it.

I recently had the honor of baptizing Me-Me. I had nothing to do with what God was doing in that relationship. It all had to do with Brian and Becky's decision to relocate. They heard the cry and moved, and now Me-Me knows Jesus and is surrounded by a loving faith community.

I don't know about you, but I think these are better stories. But Me-Me's story angers me a bit too. She was struggling, but nobody knew why. Did everyone assume that since she was a girl from the 'hood that she was supposed to struggle? No. She just needed some glasses; she couldn't see! But nobody was close enough to her to understand this. Everyone just kept assuming and passing her along; nobody cared enough to get close, to invest in her, and to listen to her.

Becky followed Jesus by changing her proximity, and the Spirit changed the world through her. That's what hope looks like lived out.

THE INCARNATION

This has happened before. This idea of relocation is not a new one. We've all greatly benefited from it.

John began his gospel with a story of relocation by saying, "The Word became flesh and made his dwelling among us" (John 1:14). As Eugene Peterson says in *The Message*, "Jesus moved into the neighborhood." I like that idea—Jesus moving into our neighborhood. Wherever we are, Jesus moved there to reach us. No matter how dangerous, he came. No matter how broken, he came. No matter what, he came . . . and dwelt.

This word *dwell* is very important. This is the same word that describes God's life-giving presence among the people from the exodus to the temple. The very presence of God is dwelling among us. And now Jesus, God in the flesh, is coming to dwell with us. God is taking on flesh. Emmanuel—God is with us. Dwelling. Living. Breathing. Touching. Jesus sold his house in the nice part of the cosmos and took on the dwelling of men and women.

Proximity.

This exchange, this relocation, cost Jesus something—it cost him his life. It was risky.

You might think it was not so risky for God to dwell in the flesh, but the very definition of flesh is equated with the possibility of failure.

Jesus could have failed. Did you think Jesus' triumph over evil was a foregone conclusion? Think again. The humanity of Jesus is just as important as the divinity of Jesus. We can't have one without the other. Both are held in tension in this divine mystery. Jesus was truly, fully, completely God, but also truly, fully, completely human. If he was truly human, he could have failed. He could have turned back. He could have sought self-satisfaction. He could have taken Satan's offer of world fame or world domination. But he didn't.

It was a risky proposition putting the future and salvation of humanity in the hands of a man. Yes, a God-man, but still flesh nonetheless. But deliverance always has to take on flesh. That's why Moses needed to go to Pharaoh. That's why Nehemiah needed to rebuild the wall. And that's why Jesus had to face evil and sin.

We have to dwell to restore—to change our proximity and make our primary place of residence among the hurt and pain. And dwelling is dangerous. When you are far away, nothing can hurt you. But when you get close, when you move into the neighborhood, you become vulnerable. You are close enough to get hurt. Just ask Jesus. Dwelling always costs us something.

My friend Ben dwells in the neighborhood. He's a tall, redheaded fellow who shops at the thrift store and writes screenplays. Not the kind of guy you typically find in the middle of the 'hood. He didn't want to relocate at first. He liked his hip East Side apartment and his East Side life. He didn't want to live in community or minister to hurting kids. He ran at first, but God didn't stop pursuing.

Finally, Ben gave in and relocated. He moved into the neighborhood. He writes about his experiences and interactions. Now he has amazing stories of redemption to tell, amazing stories of hope he witnesses every day. He writes with an edgy, honest style—one that bares his soul and others' as well. On his blog, he shared this experience:

> That afternoon, the intersection of North and Fond Du Lac Avenues was busy being the busiest intersection in

Milwaukee. Everyone was Pooh with their head in the beehive, selfish selfish selfish . . .

In the crosswalk, there was a man wearing a Packers jersey, a floral scarf on his head and carrying a single plastic white hanger. Each footstep seemed a philosophical statement: No one cares, therefore I do not care. No one honked, no one looked, no one pointed. To us he was a human construction barrel, to be avoided.

As I turned, there was a woman standing by the bus stop, not waiting for the bus. The combination of her clothes—or what was left of them—suggested a costume. I wanted to give her a ride, but I realized that might be misinterpreted by her, and the police.

Further down the street, a young couple waited to cross. She held the child like a bag of groceries and he stood five feet away like he didn't know them. The smoke from his cigarette slipped into my cracked window.

I looked into the rearview mirror and a pair of narrowed eyes looked back. I rubbed the gunk from the corners. I looked away. I looked ahead.

When I arrived at the community house, it was time for Bible Club. A boy gripped my arm like it was a branch hanging over a rushing river. "What do you think God looks like?" asked Kevin. "He's a yellow spirit," shouted one kid. "I bet he's got big sandals," shouted a second. The third was so quiet Kevin had to repeat it for us: "Maybe he looks like all of us put together."[4]

MIKRONS

At one point, the disciples, apparently dealing with competition and anxiety, asked Jesus, "Who, then, is the greatest in the kingdom of heaven?" (Matt. 18:1). This is how Matthew records Jesus' answer: "He called a little child to him, and placed the child among them. And he said: 'Truly I tell you, unless you change and become like little children, you will never enter the kingdom of heaven. Therefore, whoever takes the lowly position of this child is the greatest in the kingdom of heaven. And whoever welcomes one such child in my name welcomes me'" (Matt. 18:2–5).

Perhaps as you read this story, you envisioned Jesus sitting on a big rock with nicely combed hair and a beautiful white robe, welcoming three little white children dressed in freshly cleaned clothes, with blond hair and blue eyes, coming to sit on his lap. Is that about right? This scene is highly stylized in our minds. But we have it all wrong. The scene most likely did not look anything like this. In fact, the scene would have been heartbreaking.

You know those images on TV of kids in Central America or Africa, living in the landfills, gathering enough food to survive from the trash heap? Those kids who are covered in dirt, who have flies encircling them and barely have enough tattered clothes to cover their little bodies? That's probably closer to what the reality of the situation was for these children coming to Jesus. They were not dressed in their white "Easter best." They were probably dirty, neglected, and hungry.

Can you make that switch in your mind? If you can, then you are getting closer to understanding what Jesus was talking about in this passage. Here is a description of children at the time of Jesus that is helpful for us to better understand this scene:

> Contrary to our ethnocentric and anachronistic projections of innocent, trusting, imaginative, and delightful children playing at the knee of a gentle Jesus, childhood in antiquity was a time of terror. . . . Children were the weakest, most vulnerable members of society. Infant mortality rates sometimes reached 30 percent. Another 30 percent of live births were dead by age six, and 60 percent were gone by age sixteen. Recent estimates are that in excess of 70 percent would have lost one or both parents before reaching puberty. . . . Children were always the first to suffer from famine, war, disease, and dislocation. . . . Children had little status within the community of family. While a minor, a child was on par with a slave."[5]

This understanding changes things, doesn't it? We are no longer talking about Jesus urging the disciples to become like nice, clean, trusting, and highly valued twenty-first-century Western children. Jesus was destroying the motive for the question that was posed about who was the greatest. Jesus was challenging upward mobility and showing the disciples who is truly great.

I like what Chad Myers and Elaine Enns say about this scene in *Ambassadors of Reconciliation*:

> The disciples' initial question reflects both inward anxiety and outward conditioning concerning social positions. People in ancient Palestine assumed that prestige was a limited good, distributed according to one's station in the social hierarchy. Our modern cultural cosmology is not different in kind, only in scope: because of the possibility of social mobility, we are far more competitive. We aspire upward in a hundred ways, large and small: better degrees, bigger pulpits, more influence, higher pay, etc. But the flip side of the upward social fixation is our tendency to scapegoat downwards. We believe that those above us somehow deserve their privilege, because they are supposedly brighter, harder working, more entrepreneurial. Conversely, those below us are equally deserving of their social disadvantages, because they are allegedly lazy, dependent, incapable. Such social conditioning lies at the heart of the culture of domination, undergirding the political and economic architecture of stratification. And it is the first target of Jesus' teaching.[6]

Jesus took the disciples' question—a question about who is the greatest, a question rooted in upward aspiration, a question that at its core was a question of competition—and blew it up.

We live in a culture of competition—and that's part of why Facebook is so successful, because even if we are not aware, we are competing with one another about who has the best life. We learn early on that we have to compete with everyone around us to get ahead. This term, *get ahead*, is marinated in competition.

It implies that others are seeking what we want, and we have to get ahead of them, outsmart them, outwork them, whatever we have to do—at all costs. So we compete. There are a limited amount of resources, and we must be the best.

The other day someone told me, "I know you—you are competitive." No, I'm not all that competitive in most things in life. (Well, Carolina basketball is one exception to that.) But I *am* competitive in one distinct area—church. So when I see other churches doing amazing things and growing like crazy, I get competitive. My identity is so wrapped up in this place that I take offense. I get anxious and competitive.

But the more I take seriously the message of Jesus, the more I'm realizing that "being competitive" is just a nice, fancy way of saying, "I'm fearful." Competition is just candy-coated fear.

The reason Facebook gives me anxiety, the reason I get competitive and anxious when I see other churches doing other really cool things, is because I'm afraid. I'm afraid I'm not good enough. I'm afraid that I will lose what I have. I'm afraid that if I don't succeed—if I don't have the biggest and the best—I will be seen as a failure. I'm afraid to fail because I get my worth from what I do. What I do defines me in such a way that it has the power over me to tell me who I am. But deep down, I'm just afraid.

Living in competition is living in the wrong story. The American dream has convinced us that we need to strive to be the "greatest." That we need to climb the ladder of success and fame and money and more. But it is just a nightmare! Why do we give such credence to the American dream with its myth of upward aspiration after reading this teaching of Jesus?

When the disciples asked Jesus about who was the greatest, Jesus responded in a peculiar way. He said, "Unless you change and become like little children, you will never enter the kingdom of heaven." The word in the Greek here for "little children" or "little ones" is *mikron*.

Unless you become like mikrons, you will not enter in. The smallest. The least. The most vulnerable. The most insignificant.

So can you tell me again, why are we jumping over one another to get to the top? To get more? Apparently there's only death at the top of that ladder. Jesus is telling us that life is at the bottom—so move down.

You see, when we see the world with limited resources and only so many positions at the top, and we must "get ahead" by any means possible, then our eyes are always focused on up, more, richer, better. And when our eyes are looking up the ladder, we don't see those at the bottom of the ladder. Sure, sometimes we let the crumbs fall out of our pockets of upward pursuit, but we don't really *see* them.

If we are looking and climbing up, we can never see the true pain of those at the bottom. If all of our attention is on the accumulation of more, then we will never stop to feel the pain of the systems of injustice that are oppressing those at the bottom.

The American dream breeds competition, and competition breeds fear, and fear leads to suffering, because it creates us and them. It creates people who are always running away from suffering instead of into it, people who are so focused on "getting ahead" that we leave others behind.

RELOCATION

This is why we have to relocate. Because if we don't relocate our lives, we will never see it. If we don't relocate our desires, we will never see the people who are hurting. If we don't relocate our priorities, we will always be asking the wrong questions and missing the answers that truly give us life.

Abundant life is not at the top of the ladder of success; it is at the bottom. I know that goes against everything we've ever been taught, but that's what Jesus is teaching us.

Are we all called to relocate? Yes, absolutely we are. If we are following Jesus, then we are called to relocate our lives from the primary residence of the American dream to the primary residence of the kingdom of God. We are called to relocate our stories from the story of accumulation to the story of distribution. We are called to relocate our stories from the story of success to the story of sacrifice. We are called to relocate our stories from the story of competition to the story of compassion.

The cure for fear is downward mobility, and the only way we will be cured is to relocate. For some of us that will mean selling our homes and moving to an under-resourced community to take part in the pain, injustice, and neglect in order to dwell there and sacrifice there and welcome the little ones. For others it might mean relocating to an overseas mission field. For others, instead of always spending our free time on the lake, it may mean spending our time tutoring kids or serving a single mother.

I firmly believe God is calling so many to make this shift in their perception of reality—to relocate their homes to under-resourced neighborhoods. To become like Tom and Kelly and Brian and Becky. To become like Nehemiah. To become like Jesus.

Are all called to physically relocate? No, I don't think so. There are many people in our church who are not called to relocate. But some are. So we tell the stories of those who relocate and call them "relocators." We hold up the story high, because if we don't, it will not become normal. We want the story of relocation to become normal.

For those who are not called to move yet, they can support relocators. They can pray for them. They can continue to process relocating their desires and dreams from up to down, from greatest to least. They can decide to relocate part of their lives or make intentional decisions to relocate the dominant story of their lives from accumulation, success, and competition to distribution, sacrifice, and compassion. To make a decision to serve in different places, harder places. To open their lives to receive more "little ones." To give their money to different places.

Instead of the story of more and bigger, maybe the story we need to tell is the story of less and smaller. Maybe the story that inspires the world is not how big our churches are, but how much our churches are willing to risk. To call others into risk. To move into neighborhoods so the Word of God can take on flesh.

We need more of these stories. They are better stories anyway, because stories of love always are.

Facebook gives me anxiety because so much of it is about impressing others with our bigger lives. Facebook makes me afraid. Afraid of what I could lose or miss out on. But when I'm hanging out in an under-resourced neighborhood with people who have made intentional choices to relocate, I feel no fear because I feel no competition. They are not asking anything of me. They are not flaunting their prosperity to me. They are, rather, inviting me to join them in their vulnerable lives.

Anxiety makes us worry about what we might lose. Anxiety breeds competition and competition breeds fear. And fear produces separation. Fear always divides; it never unites. There is certainly a lot of separation in our world. Because there's so much fear.[7]

What does God say? Yep, "Do not fear." God knows something we don't. Fear will destroy our lives. It will divide us from one another, and division breeds suffering. What's the opposite of fear? Indifference? Nope.

The opposite of fear is love. John said it this way: "There is no fear in love. But perfect love drives out fear" (1 John 4:18). If we love, we will not fear. If we love, we won't make stupid statements about what we don't know to be real.

Sacrifice would have been impossible if it were not for the relocation that came first. Relocation might just be one of the highest forms of love. And love never fails. If we love, we will be dedicated to restoration. Because only when we relocate can we reconcile with those different from us. Only when we relocate can we take part in the rebuilding of the broken-down walls. Only when we relocate can we see that Jesus looks like all of us put together.

Like a bunch of mikrons.

8 DANGEROUS PRESENCE

"My name is Toby."

This classic line is from the TV miniseries based on *Roots*, Alex Haley's novel about slavery. There was a new slave on the plantation named Kunta Kinte. He was strong young man with great value to the plantation owners, but early in his stay, Kunta Kinte decided to try to escape.

He failed.

Then the slave masters tied up Kunta Kinte and began to beat him with a whip. The master asked the young man his name, and the slave responded, "Kunta Kinte."

The oppressor told him, "No, this is not your name. Your name is Toby. The master has given you the name Toby. It's a good name. Your name is Toby."

But Kunta Kinte refused to give in. He was beaten again. And again. And again.

Finally, as the slave neared his breaking point, the slave master asked him his name. This time the young man responded, "Toby. My name is Toby."

This classic scene has been both a joke and an inspiration in our culture. It has something to say to us today.

I recently visited a partner church of ours in Grand Rapids, Michigan, called The Edge. Pastor Troy Evans founded this urban church in order to impact the hip-hop culture of urban Grand Rapids. Troy is a former gang member who found redemption and renewal in Christ and is now a pastor. He founded The Edge in order to provide a culturally relevant place of worship for young men and women who love the hip-hop culture. Their worship is full of bass-driven, rhythmic rap choruses. The people worship Christ in their cultural context. It's beautiful to see.[1]

As I was experiencing worship at The Edge, Pastor Troy reminded me of this scene in *Roots* and its connection with the story of Daniel in the Bible.

When we read the prophecy of Daniel, most of us focus on the beasts and dragons and destruction Daniel described. Most of us focus on Daniel's apocalypse, or unveiling, and miss the main point. The book opens by reminding the reader of the situation. Babylon and its pagan army had destroyed Jerusalem and left it in ashes. Babylon plundered the land, taking for itself the good and valuable, including the people. Daniel begins like this:

> In the third year of the reign of Jehoiakim king of Judah, Nebuchadnezzar king of Babylon came to Jerusalem and besieged it. And the Lord delivered Jehoiakim king of Judah into his hand, along with some of the articles from the temple of God. These he carried off to the temple of

> his god in Babylonia and put in the treasure house of his god. Then the king ordered Ashpenaz, chief of his court officials, to bring into the king's service some of the Israelites from the royal family and the nobility—young men without any physical defect, handsome, showing aptitude for every kind of learning, well informed, quick to understand, and qualified to serve in the king's palace. He was to teach them the language and literature of the Babylonians. The king assigned them a daily amount of food and wine from the king's table. They were to be trained for three years, and after that they were to enter the king's service. (Dan. 1:1–5)

Slaves. Babylon took slaves and trained them so they could use them for the purposes of Babylon's kingdom. Israel again found itself in exile, enslaved.

Babylon was an oppressive force, taking the good of another land in order to benefit itself. But in order to use the good of another land—in order to put slaves in the king's service—Babylon would first have to break these Israelites. They had to break them of their old allegiances and worldview, from eating their old food, and from worshiping their old God, Yahweh. That breaking always culminates in a new name. The old name—the birth name—is no longer valid. It reminds them of their homeland, their old allegiances, their old lives.

Remembering the past gives hope for the future. Oppressors want to vanquish the past, and with it, all future chances of hope.

They say that God is no longer your ruler; we are, and so you need a new name. Forget your old name and the significance of what that name stood for . . . we will give you a name that means nothing.

That's just what Babylon did to these exiles—they gave them new names. "Among those who were chosen were some from Judah: Daniel, Hananiah, Mishael and Azariah. The chief official gave them new names: to Daniel, the name Belteshazzar; to Hananiah, Shadrach; to Mishael, Meshach; and to Azariah, Abednego" (Dan. 1:6–7).

In Hebrew, the name Daniel means "God is my Judge." Daniel's name reminded him that God is the one who would make all things right, that God is in charge of the universe, and that Daniel's life was lived before that Judge. The Babylonian name Beltheshazzar means "prince of Bel." Prince, servant, ambassador of the Babylonian god Bel.

The oppressors were attempting to give Daniel a new identity. They were attempting to break Daniel. They were trying to give him a new purpose, not a purpose to serve God, but a purpose to serve the empire. Why would they want to do this? Because an allegiance to God is dangerous to the empire and the king. So empires—or any oppressive force—always sought to wipe out allegiances that compete with their goals. This begins with the name.

This is why the New Testament says over and over again, "Jesus is Lord." So if Jesus is Lord, that means Caesar is not Lord. Allegiances must always be in the proper place. That's why the kingdom of God and any other kingdom are incompatible.

The values of the kingdom of God are not compatible with the values of the kingdom of America or the kingdom of Russia or the kingdom of China. This is exactly why Paul said over and over again that Jesus is Lord. It's offensive and threatening to anyone who calls Caesar Lord.

God wants all of us. The first commandment, "Worship and serve the Lord your God" (see Ex. 20:3), is about allegiances. God was saying to the people, I want your allegiance, and if your allegiance is to me, then it can't be to anyone else. That's why you can't have any other gods or any idols. You belong to me, and if you belong to me you can't belong to anyone else.

It's like a marriage. If you are married, then you can't flirt with other people, have sex with other people, or seek your emotional comfort in other people. Your heart belongs to your wife or husband, and to give it to another is to betray your love.

We live in a world of competing allegiances. Apple wants your allegiance. Google wants it. Facebook wants it. McDonald's, Wendy's, Republicans, and Democrats all want it. Everyone is fighting over who you will be loyal to, who you will give your heart and money to. We look at these things as simple products, but products can quickly turn into idols if we are not careful.

The message of Scripture from beginning to end declares loud and clear that our allegiances—all of them—belong to God. Jesus is Lord. And if Jesus is Lord, then no one else is. If Jesus is Lord, then nothing else is. Not the president. Not the military. Not the economy. Not the American dream. Not my career. Not my safety. Not my education. Not my retirement fund. Jesus. That's it.

Now, this is quite easy for me to write on a piece of paper or preach in a sermon, but it's much harder to live it out. In real life, this gets tricky. How do we give our allegiance to Jesus when every other thing around us is pulling and vying for our loyalty? How do we call Jesus Lord and serve in the military? How do we call Jesus Lord and serve in politics? How do we call Jesus Lord and work for a CEO or be the CEO? How do we call Jesus Lord and eat dinner?

It's not always clear cut. How do we live "in the world" but not become "of the world"? How do we participate in the economy and protect ourselves from worshiping the economy? How do we buy products but not become slaves to them or make those who produce them our slaves?

The most common reaction is for people to trivialize this and stop trying to hold these two together. They live their lives and go to church on Sunday, making the message of Jesus an entirely "spiritual" experience that has little implication for the physical real world. Jesus is "Lord of my heart" but not "Lord of my life," so to speak.

Another reaction is to completely withdraw from culture and all of its complexity. This is a less-common reaction but still one that has occurred in the course of history. I'm certainly not a fan of withdrawal, but I'm not a fan of relativism either. I think the answer is found in the difficult maze of choices we must make while living day to day within a culture of idolatry.

Do I buy that product produced by oppression? Do I eat that chocolate made from beans picked by child slaves? Do I take that job that will work me to death but provide the income necessary for my dreams to come true?

These are tough questions. Thankfully, Jesus is full of grace. We will make missteps more than not, but the real test of whether we are in the world and not of the world is in the struggle.

Are we struggling to reconcile our faith in Jesus with the products we buy? Or the jobs we work? Or the way we use our money or time? We must struggle with these decisions and put everything under the lordship of Jesus.

To struggle is to be engaged. This is why when God encountered Jacob, God gave Jacob the new name, Israel, which means "one who struggles with God" (see Gen. 32:27–29). If we don't care, we don't struggle; we just do whatever we want or whatever makes us feel good.

Continuing in the story of Daniel, we read something brilliant. Daniel may have been living in exile, in the empire of the oppressors. He may have been trained by them, given a new name by them, and forced to serve them, but he didn't lose his allegiance to God. He lived within the empire but subverted the empire. He subtly stood against the challenge of Babylon to change his allegiances. How? He didn't eat their food:

> But Daniel resolved not to defile himself with the royal food and wine, and he asked the chief official for permission not to defile himself this way. Now God had caused the official to show favor and compassion to Daniel, but the official told Daniel, "I am afraid of my lord the king, who has assigned your food and drink. Why should he see you looking worse than the other young men your age? The king would then

> have my head because of you." Daniel then said to the guard whom the chief official had appointed over Daniel, Hananiah, Mishael and Azariah, "Please test your servants for ten days: Give us nothing but vegetables to eat and water to drink. Then compare our appearance with that of the young men who eat the royal food, and treat your servants in accordance with what you see." So he agreed to this and tested them for ten days. At the end of the ten days they looked healthier and better nourished than any of the young men who ate the royal food. So the guard took away their choice food and the wine they were to drink and gave them vegetables instead. (Dan. 1:8–16)

The four of them didn't eat the royal food. We might think that they looked good because they ate vegetables. We all want to look good and be thin, so we resolve to eat like Daniel did, so we come up with the "Daniel fast."[2] But this is about keeping our allegiance with God, refusing to get comfortable in exile, and refusing to take their nice food that seems so tempting, but in the end will begin to chip away at our commitment to living out the message of Jesus.

I've had people say to me, "I've been offered this great job. I will be making so much more money. They want me to work a lot more hours, but that's OK, right? I will be able to support my family in a greater way, get out of debt, and give so much more money to church." Then I see the result, which usually looks something like this: The job consumes them; they don't have any time for their kids or their family; they are so busy that they stop going to church or stop volunteering; they buy a bigger house and more expensive cars, and now they have to work even more to sustain the lifestyle they have opened for themselves. They become slaves, living in exile. The empire dangled a carrot and they bit into it . . . and died.

You can plug in a scenario here; there are many different ones. They usually end in the same way. When we give our allegiance to something other than Jesus, we lose our lives. Daniel would not eat the food of Babylon. He refused to get comfortable in his exile. He kept his edge. He did not let the empire steal his memories of what he was committed to, where he was from, and whom he served. The vegetables did not make him look better. The passion for God living inside him, his memory of his allegiance to God's ways, and living in exile but dreaming of freedom was what made him look better to the Babylonians.

Hope of Yahweh lived within Daniel, and the Babylonians had never seen this before. (The hope of Jesus living in you looks this way too.) They thought it was the vegetables. Sometimes we think it's the vegetables, but it's really the passion for God living in us and the refusal to give in to the oppression of the evil forces around us.

The Babylonians eventually caught on to this subversion. They realized that they had not broken Daniel and that he was not giving in. We can't keep our allegiance to God a secret; it will always be revealed. We will be forced to choose what or whom we will worship sooner or later. That's when things become dangerous. Our choices always have consequences.

The king of Babylon set up a golden image to be worshiped, but the faithful Jews refused to worship the idol. You may know the story of Shadrach, Meshach, and Abednego. When they came before the king to defend their allegiance to the God of Israel, facing execution in a fiery furnace, they said, "If we are thrown into the blazing furnace, the God we serve is able to deliver us from it, and he will deliver us from Your Majesty's hand. But even if he does not, we want you to know, Your Majesty, that we will not serve your gods or worship the image of gold you have set up" (Dan. 3:17–18).

Maybe we need to take a stand like this in our own culture. Instead of bowing down to the idols of success, power, and convenience, maybe we need to say, "Your Majesty, sorry, but we will not buy those products made by slaves, vote for people forgetting about the poor, or exchange money for time."

The king did not like this answer, so he threw them into the fiery furnace. Absolute power cannot tolerate opposition. But an interesting thing happened: They didn't burn up. And then something even more amazing happened: Another person showed up. There were not just three of them; now there were four in the furnace.

Jesus doesn't usually get us out of danger in a flash, but one thing is for sure: He will always be with us in that danger. He will never leave us. He will always show up.

The king was amazed to see four men in the furnace, so he opened it, and they walked out. Their clothes didn't even smell like smoke. God was glorified, and the whole kingdom knew that the God of Israel was real.

When the followers or God take a stand for what we believe and declare to the false gods of this world, "We will not worship you. Do what you may, but we will not worship you!"—then people will know God is real. Following Jesus should cost us something. What is it costing you?

Later on, Daniel was caught praying to the God of Israel even though a decree had been made that for thirty days prayers could only be offered to the king of Babylon. Daniel knew the consequences; he prayed anyway. He refused to forget what his real name meant. He refused to forget who his allegiance belonged to. No matter the consequences, he knew that to worship the idols meant to lose his soul. Babylon would have stolen it, and that was worse than death.

Daniel was thrown into a cage of lions, presumably to be eaten alive. The king threw him in. Nothing happened, and Daniel walked out. God was glorified again, and the whole kingdom knew that the God of Israel was real.

You see, the book of Daniel is not about the end times; it's about the now times. It's about how we live as exiles in the face of opposition and persecution. When we are forced to choose between God and the empire, what will we choose?

Every day we have to make choices about what we are going to live for—about whom or what we are going to worship. Are we going to worship money? The pursuit of more? That's what the world wants us to worship. It looks so good; it seems so right. And a little money won't hurt, right? Will we choose to live in safety and comfort, even if that means neglecting the teachings, messages, and commandments of our Lord? If we neglect these, is he really our Lord? Or is something else lord? Ourselves? Our job? Our career? Our future? Where is our allegiance?

Don't get me wrong; I'm not against money. If you can make it, make it. But don't worship it. There's a difference.

There's a married couple in our church who are both doctors. Most doctors I know work all the time and make quite a bit of money. Most doctors are brilliant people, and this couple is no different, but they have surprised me. They have the ability to make a lot of money, but she has made the intentional choice to work only part time at a family practice so she can be at home with her young children. He has made the intentional choice to make sure that serving and being involved in a local church is a priority in their lives, and so he sets boundaries with his schedule.

There's a lawyer in our church who is finishing up a clerkship working under a judge. She's brilliant and everyone knows it. She had the choice of working for nearly any law firm in the city and making a nice living for herself. She has a ton of student loans that need to be paid off, but she made a choice to live for something else. She made the choice to accept the position of the executive director of an organization to help sexually exploited girls find hope and freedom. She makes about a tenth of what she could make otherwise.

Again, money is not the issue here. But there's a difference between making it and worshiping it.

BROKEN LEGS

There is a family who recently began attending our church. They have three little girls. They felt God was leading them out of their suburban life and into the city. We began to talk about relocation, and they got excited. Then we began working with them on a plan to relocate, and they put their house on the market. They were ready to move.

Then the world around them fell apart. They began to experience stress in every part of their lives. Their jobs became increasingly difficult. Their girls began to get sick. Their marriage began to see increased tension. They were blindsided and suffering. They told me that they would move when God sold their house and opened up a door for them to walk through. I warned them about dictating what God must do in order for them to follow his call. I told them that if they knew God was calling them to do this, then they needed to do it regardless of the financial circumstance they were moving under. Sometimes we tell God that if he does this and this and this, then we will do this. Maybe we should just do what God wants us to do and let him figure it all out.

They were wavering in their decision to relocate. Their house wasn't selling. In fact, no one was even looking at it. Then one of their daughters, who was three years old, broke her femur. That's a serious break. A break that could change a kid's life.

That's the last time I ever talked to them. They told me that was it. They couldn't take any more. I felt such compassion for them. I think I might have changed my mind too if I was in their situation.

Maybe for the first time in their lives, they were beginning to make decisions not based on what was best for them or their family, not on how much money they could make or the arc of their career path. Rather, they were making a step to change their allegiance. No longer were they going to live and worship the god of money and comfort. They were making an intentional choice to follow Jesus into a hard and difficult place.

One thing we must remember is that evil is real, and those powers do not like when we begin to change our allegiance from greed to generosity, from self-satisfaction to sacrifice, from selfishness to love. The empire of evil sees what is happening, and it reacts with all of its ugly force. Evil saw what this family was doing, how they were going to relocate to be rebuilders—how they were going to relocate to bring glory to God—and the evil forces did not like it. So the forces rose up against them. This family got hit hard.

As I reflected, I realized that much of this was my fault. When I met them and they told me their desires, I was eager—too eager—for them to jump in. I failed them. This is difficult stuff, and they needed more prayer partners around them. They needed more people holding them up and encouraging them, and they had not spent enough time building the foundation for this huge step of relocation in their lives. They jumped in too far too fast, and I let them do it. As their pastor, I should have cautioned them—told them to just sit in our church for a year, to build relationships, to build a prayer network around them, to network with people who had done this already.

Don't do these things alone. Gather people around you to pray for you and hold you up. Connect yourself to a local church that values relocation and reconciliation, and sit under them and allow them to cover and bless you. All too often I see passionate young people charge out all alone without the partnership of a local church, and they end up being burned out and done in one year. Everything said in this book must be understood as coming from within the local church, from its blessing and its covering over your life. There are no lone rangers. This is serious business, and it is not to be taken lightly.

I'm not sure where you stand on evil. I'll tell you where I stand. It's real, and it stands to bring oppression, injustice, pain, suffering, hurt, and destruction wherever it can. And any system or person is capable of giving itself to evil. Every time a government, corporation, business, or even person uses a God-centered calling for a human-diminishing activity, they become a partner with evil. Every created thing is called to glorify God—government, business, people.

But remember that everything is redeemable. Evil understands this, I think. When we begin to make choices to fight injustice and oppression, when we make choices to put God's desires above our own, when we make choices to live for something bigger than ourselves, then evil fights back. And it fights back hard.

In his book *The Powers That Be*, Walter Wink describes this:

> When the Powers That Be catch the merest whiff of God's new order, they automatically mobilize all their might to crush it. Even before the full fury of the Powers was unleashed on Jesus, he apparently predicted the outcome of the confrontation. The Powers are so immense, and the opposition so weak, that every attempt at fundamental change seems doomed to failure. Merely winning does not satisfy the Powers; they must win big, in order to demoralize opposition before it can gain momentum. Gratuitous violence, mocking derision, and intimidating brutality in the means of execution typify the Powers—all this is standard, unexceptional. Jesus died just like all the others who challenged the world-dominating Powers.[3]

When we challenge the systems of oppression and injustice of this world, when we make even the slightest changes in our lives to live out the message of Jesus in practical ways, then the powers of this world will come against us. This is a given. This is why so many people stop. They've been living in their own dreams for so long, simply asking God to bless their lives, that when they wake up and begin to try to live out God's desire for their lives, they wish they would just go back to sleep. They think the whole world looks different, and they aren't sure they want to live in this world. They liked their nightmares better than this current reality.[4] They'd like to go back to sleep.

But the question that arises from this is inevitable: Why does evil—the powers, empire, whatever you want to call it—rise up against us when we begin to really, truly live out and make decisions based on the life and teachings of Jesus? Why do they fight so hard against us?

Because we are dangerous to their regime and their future. When we truly live out the message of Jesus, worship God alone, and put the full force of our passion behind our allegiance to Jesus and not ourselves, then we take on a power that is dangerous to every human-diminishing, oppressive, evil force in this universe.

We become a dangerous presence.

It is exactly when we choose to put our lives and our futures at risk, because of our commitment to the kingdom of God, that we become a danger to the oppressive forces of this world. We put our lives in danger, and we become dangerous.

When we are faced with being thrown into the furnace or the lions' den, God moves in amazing ways around us. When we are faced with putting our careers or financial security or physical security in danger by radically living out the message of Jesus, by relocating or pouring out our lives or getting involved with the poor and oppressed, God becomes so real to us, maybe for the first time. This is when we see God's glory on display before us, fighting for us on our behalf and on behalf of the marginalized.

The church loses its witness when we choose to eat the fruit of the empire and the world around us, and so we never get the opportunity to stand before the powers of this world and say, "I refuse to worship you and your gods of stone and paper. I serve the living God, the King of Kings, and God has called me to give my life on behalf of the hurting and hopeless. Do your worst! My allegiances are to the kingdom of the living God!"

In those moments, God becomes real to us. In those moments, the whole world sees our commitment to our Lord, and the whole world sees who is really in charge. Not Caesar. Not the king of Babylon. Not Wall Street. Not the Pentagon. Jesus.

I truly believe that if more of us who professed to follow Christ would put off our selfish desires and move our lives and our attention into places that are risky for our lives, then the church would grow in amazing ways.

If people would choose to move into under-resourced and crime-ridden neighborhoods and get involved with their neighbors, stand with their neighbors, hold the police and city officials accountable to engage these forgotten neighborhoods, put our kids in city schools and get involved in those schools, refusing to buy into the lie of the oppressive forces that these kids aren't smart enough, then our churches would grow and burst at the seams. People would be clamoring to get in, because they would see that we put others first, that we are taking a stand for what we believe. People would see that we are people of love. People would see that even though everyone else forgot them, Jesus hasn't. We might get thrown into the furnace, but someone else will be there with us. Jesus will be there, and everyone will see and glorify God.

But those choices come with consequences. The powers don't like these choices, and they will seek with all they are to break us.

KUNTA KINTE

The oppressive forces of this world want to give us new names, like Selfish, Greedy, Lazy, Fearful, Angry, Racist, Addict, etc. When we make an attempt to refuse the power of the empire and to live for Jesus in radical and self-sacrificing ways, the whole force of evil will come against us. Prepare yourself. It will not be easy. This is why you need a church around you. You might get beaten. You might lose something. You might break your leg. That's the brutal reality to this fight. Jesus was murdered. So were the disciples. So are many missionaries today.

Following Jesus is not easy. It never has been. It was never meant to be. It will always cost us something.

C. S. Lewis said, "I didn't go to religion to make me happy. I always knew a bottle of Port would do that. If you want a religion to make you feel really comfortable, I certainly don't recommend Christianity."[5] Following Jesus is not comfortable. It's like sleeping on rocks on the ground in the African bush. But Jesus is there, and where else would we want to be?

So when we make those choices, when we become a dangerous presence, when the force of evil comes against us, let us not take the name they have desired to give us. Let us not believe for a moment that our names are Selfish or Fearful. We are servants of the Creator of the universe. Our names are Beloved. Our names are Called. Our names are Sent. Our names are Ones who Sacrifice. Our names are Restorers.

Our names are not Toby; our names are Kunta Kinte. Our names are Followers of the Resurrected Jesus. We are called Christians! Jesus was a dangerous presence, and so are we.

9

IDIOTS

For our tenth wedding anniversary, my wife and I went to Puerto Rico. On the beach, sitting in my blue beach chair, I began to read Fyodor Dostoyevsky's novel *The Idiot*. I love Dostoyevsky's writing because of the way he weaves his struggles and reflections of theology and God's work in the world into his literature.

The Idiot is set in eighteenth-century Russia at the height of the aristocracy. The main characters, all aristocratic, are constantly jostling for higher standing in society and fighting for new ways to get more money.

The main character, "the idiot," inherits a great deal of wealth. But he is completely out of place in the aristocratic society in which he finds himself. He is sick, frail, and does not understand the social cues of high society. He is completely out of place. He always says and does the wrong things. And strangely, he does not seem to care about his wealth. But his most defining trait is the way he cares for those around him. Even when they hurt him or make fun of him, he keeps caring.

This man loves a beautiful woman, who intentionally injures and thwarts her pursuers as a hobby. She is cruel and vain, but the idiot loves her nonetheless. He loves her for what he sees in her. Somewhere in the depths of her soul, he sees her goodness, humility, and compassion. She continues to hurt him, and he continues to pursue her.

In the end, the idiot is in a mental institution, an asylum. In Russian the word *idiot* does not mean "not smart" but rather mentally ill, unstable, out of touch with reality.

We will come back to this later . . .

AGAPISM

Nicholas Wolterstorff, a professor of philosophy at Yale University, writes and thinks in a somewhat controversial manner. I love what he says about the message of Scripture in relation to justice:

> Slowly I began to see that the Bible is a book about justice; but what a strange and haunting form of justice! Not our familiar modern Western justice of no one invading one's right to determine one's life as one will. Rather the justice of the widow, the orphan, and the alien. A society is just when all the little ones, all the defenseless ones, all the unprotected ones, have been brought back into community. Biblical justice is the shepherd leaving the corral to look for the hundredth one and then throwing a feast when the one is found.[1]

In his book *Justice in Love*, Wolterstorff lays out the connection between love, what he describes as *agapism*, and justice.[2] *Justice*, as defined by Wolterstorff, is the intention and process that results in the defenseless and unprotected ones in society being brought back into community, where they can be protected and cared for.

Professor Wolterstorff is not the first one to speak in these terms. A young Jewish rabbi by the name of Yeshua spoke this way as well. At one point, just before the now famous parable of the good Samaritan, a religious scholar asked the rabbi, "Who then is my neighbor?" The religious scholar knew he was commanded to love his neighbor, but the true question was in the details—exactly who is *my neighbor*? We ask this question today, don't we? Even if we don't realize it. We might say, "Who am I responsible for? My family? My friends? Just myself? Or are there others for whom I am responsible?"

These are big questions. Questions that make us uncomfortable. If we are responsible for others, their well-being is connected to our well-being. Their future is connected to our future. If we are responsible for others, their lack will be our lack. Right? I am a father of two children. I am responsible for them. If they suffer, I will suffer. If they are in pain, I will be in pain. Their future affects my future. Their well-being affects my well-being. So, if I am responsible for my community, then when those in my community suffer, I suffer. Or have you been so isolated from your neighbor that you don't even realize the reason you are suffering is due to their suffering? Or do you not even realize you are suffering?

Jesus responds to this question of "Who is my neighbor?" with a striking parable that is woven into our modern-day consciousness. Jesus started his story with an attention-grabber. He put a nameless, faceless individual who had been beaten and robbed on the side of a certain road. But this road was not just any road; it was one of the busiest arteries to the "suburbs" that also happened to be a dangerous road to travel. Criminals would hang out behind rocks and curves to jump out and mug passersby. It was a bloody road, and everyone knew it. That's why Jesus used this road as the setting for his story.

At the beginning of the parable, the man was lying half dead and bleeding on the side of the road. His ID and clothes had been stolen. There was no way to identify him. Was he an undocumented worker? Was he wealthy? Did he live in the 'hood? We don't know. Jesus intentionally left this a mystery in his story. The man could have been anyone. Could be us. Could be our brother or our son. Or someone we don't even know. Could be someone we hate.

Jesus created conflict in his parable by introducing a priest who passed by this unidentified man. Surely the priest would stop, right? Nope. The priest "passed by on the other side of the road." More likely at the time, the priest probably had to step over this hurting, unidentified man because the roads weren't that wide.

How often do we step over the hurting, the oppressed, the dying, because we don't want to trouble ourselves? We think someone else will help. How often do we say a prayer: "God, please send someone to help this poor soul." Maybe God looks down at us and thinks, "I just sent you!"

But what is more remarkable is that the priest was justified in this action. If the priest would have touched the man who was bleeding, the priest would have been defiled and become ceremonially unclean and could not offer his priestly service to the people until after he went through the ritual cleansing process. The people would not get their sermon or be offered Communion.

Then came a Levite, also a religious leader. Levites aided in the functions of the temple. They worked in church. We might call them associate pastors or lay leaders today. The same thing that applied to the priest applied to the Levite. The church workers would have nothing to do with this man who was dying on the side of the street. They were worried more about themselves than they were about this man. Churches still struggle with this, don't we?

Then comes the hero of the story: a Samaritan. I will not dwell on the point here but the Jews hated Samaritans. The Samaritan cared for the wounded man. He poured oil and wine on his wounds. Oil and wine were considered medication. They were also elements used in the temple worship.[3] The real conflict is the central question: What does it mean to worship God? How are oil and wine best used? In a church service or to mend wounds? Who is really worshiping God—the priests and Levites with their sacred duties in the temple with oil and wine, or the Samaritan serving the man on the road? Is worship singing, preaching, and taking Communion, or is it something more?

Jesus finished his story by telling the audience that the Samaritan put up the injured man in a hotel and gave the clerk money to pay for any more expenses. The Samaritan was worshiping God. The Samaritan was risking his ritual cleanliness, safety, and financial security by taking care of this man, because the Samaritan knew he was responsible for this hurting man on the side of the road. The Samaritan knew the hurting man's well-being was tied to his.

In the end, Jesus asked the original question back to the expert in the law: "'Which of these three do you think was a neighbor to the man who fell into the hands of robbers?' The expert in the law replied, 'The one who had mercy on him.' Jesus told him, 'Go and do likewise'" (Luke 10:36–37; see 10:25–37 for the whole story).

Jesus was saying, "Go care for others, anyone in your life who needs caring for. Care for them. Bandage and put medicine in their wounds. Use your own money on their behalf. It doesn't matter who it is, doesn't matter what color their skin is—care for them. Always. Seeking their benefit above your own." This is the point of the story.

But look at verse 33: "But a Samaritan, as he traveled, came where the man was; and when he saw him, he took pity on him." There's a word that doesn't make any sense there—*pity*. The Greek word used here is *splagchnizomai*, which means "to be moved as to one's bowels," meaning that something is making such an impression on you that it is moving your soul, churning your stomach, breaking your heart, and forcing you to move into action. What you are witnessing demands action, and if you don't act, you won't be able to live with yourself. You won't be able to sleep at night. It means your heart is being broken, and in that moment, you can't not act. This *splagchnizomai* is surrounded in love. Your heart is not hard like those of the priest and Levite, who simply stepped over the wounded man. You are not seeking the benefit of yourself. You must help this person—no matter what it takes.

That's not pity. That's compassion.

When I think of pity, I think of the American tourist who is visiting India on an all-expense-paid vacation to see all the famous sights and who comes across a begging child whose family lives on two dollars a day, lives in the slums of Calcutta, and who is wearing rags to cover his sun-scorched skin and says, "Oh, that poor child. We should do something to help. Lord, have mercy on this poor little precious soul." The tourist pulls out one tiny, worthless rupee and gives it to the boy and thinks, "What a terrible country to live in."

Pity implies superiority. Pity puts the giver over and above the receiver. Pity says, "You are less than me, but out of the kindness of my heart, I will give you a gift that shows just how low you are and how high I am." Pity helps us sleep at night. It helps us quickly forget the plight of others. Pity is not for the benefit of the other; it's for the benefit of ourselves. Pity gives the little boy a rupee and then rushes off to buy lunch at the local restaurant, souvenirs to give to friends back home, and some Indian gold that will never be used again. Pity cleanses the conscience. Pity is not love. Pity does not move our bowels. Pity does not move us to action. Pity is not *splagchnizomai*.

A lot of our mission projects are rooted in pity. We feel sorry for people, so we want to do something to help. We feel guilty that we have so much, so we form a group and head to some under-resourced location to "help." We take with us our superior ways, money, and ideas. We go to "fix" the situation people are in. When we go into places with an idea of fixing something, it implies that we are superior and know how to fix it. That we are saviors. That we have things figured out, and they don't.

Many short-term mission experiences, whether in our cities or other nations, are full of pity. Granted, short-term experiences led by thoughtful and experienced leaders who understand the dynamics of under-resourced communities and nations can be positive, life-changing experiences. Unfortunately, more often than not, our mission experiences are simply throwing "good intention" darts at a wall; they often leave natives full of holes.

Love demands more than pity. Love demands self-sacrifice. Wolterstorff's *agapism*, self-sacrificing love in action that helps others' lives to flourish, is a constant pouring out of one's time, talents, resources, knowledge, money, and future for the benefit of the other. Love is care. Like we would care for a loved one, for a sister or brother, for a daughter or son, for a long-time friend, or for a father or mother. That's love. Wolterstorff describes it by saying, "Love as care satisfies the criteria proposed for an adequate understanding of *agape* in the New Testament. Care includes seeking that the beloved be treated justly. And care is the sort of love that is typical of love for oneself, that Jesus attributed to God for us, and that Jesus enjoins on us for God and for neighbor."[4] To care, we must see the other as one for whom we are responsible. To care, we have to be willing to pour our lives out for the benefit of the other.

The apostle Paul said it this way: "But even if I am being poured out like a drink offering on the sacrifice and service coming from your faith . . ." (Phil. 2:17). Paul's readers would have understood what Paul was talking about. It was customary for pagan Romans to pour out a glass of wine as a sacrifice or homage to the pagan Roman gods. Paul was saying that his life was being poured out for them, for God, for the kingdom, as a sacrifice. This is love. To live lives poured out for one another.

God's resources are not limited; they are abundant. Jesus said, "What good will it be for someone to gain the whole world, yet forfeit their soul?" (Matt. 16:26). We are losing our souls, because we have so much and we are not letting it out. We are hoarders—of stuff and possessions, but also of time and talents.

Is your life a swamp with stagnant water? Or is your life like a river with water flowing? Are your blessings, time, knowledge, and talent becoming stagnant because you're hoarding them, or are they a river flowing out and providing life to others? We are called to pour out our lives—our talent, money, knowledge, and time. We are called to let our lives flow like a river.

There's a simple word we like to use for this idea of "pouring out": *redistribution*. I know this word comes with baggage. Let's get rid of that baggage. As Americans, we don't like this word, because we don't want anyone telling us that we have to give up our stuff to someone else. We don't like taxes. We don't like intrusion. We don't like anyone invading our "personal space" and taking what is ours. So we have linked this word with socialism, the dreaded idea that stands in direct opposition to our beloved capitalism.[5] When we think of redistribution, we might think of Lenin's Russia, Castro's Cuba, or socialist Norway. And we don't like it.

But *redistribution* is not a political word. Church, this is our word. Before any country or economic policy used this word, it was ours. At the beginning of the church, the early followers of Jesus valued redistribution. Acts tells us that "all the believers were together and had everything in common. They sold property and possessions to give to anyone who had need" (Acts 2:44–45). They based this on the Old Testament idea of the Year of Jubilee. Jesus declared that he was ushering in the Year of Jubilee, the Year of the Lord. Well, what do you think happened in the Year of Jubilee? Redistribution. Those who had nothing were given back what was theirs. Those who had too much gave to those who didn't have enough. This is not socialism. This is God's dream for humanity.

When we see a kid who can't read, it should shake us to our core, shake our bowels, in such a way that we redistribute our knowledge to him or her to tutor and teach that child to read. When we see a neighborhood rotting because of neglect and the people who are living there suffering because they have no advocates, we should empower them to demand that the city engage in that neighborhood and improve it. When we see kids who can't get dental care because state insurances don't provide dental benefits, then we should gather all the dentists we know and bug them until they agree to open a free dental clinic for kids in town. When we see men who are out of work, we shouldn't complain about them or make jokes about them. Rather, we should dream of new ways to get jobs into our communities. We should provide job-training skills at our churches and places of business. We should hire some under-employable people at our small businesses instead of seeking to wring profit out of every transaction.

Caring is seeking justice. Not justice to put someone in jail for some crime they committed. Rather, caring is justice that makes the world right again. Justice is partnering with God to bring shalom to the world. Peace. Seeing the world as it ought to be, not the way that it is. Lesslie Newbigin says it this way:

> Any talk of salvation apart from action for the liberation of the exploited is false. It is part of a false theology that is determined by an idealist philosophy and not by the revelation of God as he is the in the Bible. Wherever we look in the Old Testament we find that the prophets and psalmists speak of salvation in terms of actual historic happenings: deliverance from famine, sickness, danger, enemies, and oppression. Therefore, for the biblical writers, to "know the Lord" is not a matter of intellectual contemplation or mystical union; it is a matter of doing justice and mercy in concrete situations. . . . Those who claim to know the Lord but do evil are deceived. They are far from God. And the same teaching is given in the New Testament.

> There is no knowledge of God apart from the love of God, and there is no love of God apart from the love of the neighbor. "[Whoever] does not love does not know God" (1 John 4:8).
>
> Love and justice are distinct concepts, but where justice is denied love is certainly denied. If the economic order is such that the owners of land and capital can and do exploit and oppress the workers, then the commandment of love must mean more than marginal acts of personal charity; it must mean action to end exploitation. It must mean actions for liberation of which the Exodus is the model, and this must mean taking the side of the exploited and fighting against the exploiter. Fundamental to the theology of liberation is the refusal to allow a separation between truth and actions.[6]

Love is caring. Caring enough to see that I am responsible for my neighbor. I can't get out of it. Can't scoot around it. If my neighbor is being oppressed or is hungry, or if my neighbor's daughter is getting pimped out, that's not just their problem; it's my problem. That's my responsibility.

That's love. Where justice is denied, love is certainly denied.

But who is our neighbor? Everyone. Everywhere. The whole of humanity. Whoever you come across on the road of your life.

Do you see now why we move away from the pain? So we won't have to see it. So we won't have to deal with it. So we won't ever be faced with the reality that my neighbor is sinning against my other neighbor. It's easier to move away. But that's not love. That's fear, and perfect love casts out all fear.

Love is caring. Love is redistribution. But to redistribute, we have to open our eyes and see the abundance we are hoarding for ourselves. We also have to change our proximity to injustice. We have to get closer in order to give, because we only get closer when we don't fear any longer. That means we are loving. We can't simply go on a day trip into the city, feel a little pity, paint someone's porch, and call it a nice life. Nope. We have to get closer. We have to put people in our arms, bandage their brokenness, pour oil and wine over their wounds, put ourselves lower, serve the world, take out our own money, and care for others.

Pity is not love, but neither is charity. Charity (as we define it today) is the outflowing of pity. Sure, charity has its place, but let's not confuse charity with love. Love demands more. Charity can be toxic, but love never fails. Charity keeps its distance, doesn't get too involved, gives gifts that don't bring sacrifice to the giver, but rather make the giver feel good about life. Love gets close. Love gets into the mess and pain. Charity doesn't relocate; it keeps the same structures in place. But love moves into the neighborhood and takes on the role of a servant. Love moves from the role of a teacher to the role of a learner. Love moves from the role of a giver to the role of a taker. Love moves from the role of the talker to the role of the listener. Love relocates. It exchanges one place for another, one role for the other.

SUCCESS

As I was writing this book, I had many people read it over and give me their feedback. One piece of feedback I received was very interesting to me. I was told by several people that the book needed more success stories. People love to hear stories of transformation.

I get asked all the time to tell about our stories of success when I am invited to speak. Why is success so important?

In the parable of the good Samaritan, there is no mention of success. We are not told if the injured man lives or dies. We have no insight into his fate. It almost doesn't matter in this parable. Success played no part in this story.

But it plays a great part in our lives. In our industrialized Western world, profit is the standard of value. How much profit we generate dictates our value in society. What is the first thing you ask someone when you meet them for the first time? Most of the time it's something like, "What do you do?" Meaning, what is your career? Where do you work?

Do you ever think about why we ask this question? It is not just an icebreaker. There's more to it than that. We ask this question because we have to fit people into a category of evaluation. Is this person standing before me better or worse than me? Is she more valuable or less valuable? Should I look up to or down on him? And all our categories have to do with one thing: profit. How much profit a person can generate defines his or her worth in our industrialized human evaluation system. Granted, there are exceptions, like specific knowledge or ability, but generally this is the rule.

When you meet a doctor, lawyer, and CEO, what do you think of them? Compare that to the times you meet a janitor, auto mechanic, and fast-food employee. You may think less of them because they have less ability to generate profit.

Is this screwed up? Yes. But it's the reality of our delusion. And the worst of all people? The industrial bottom feeders. Those who cannot generate any profit for themselves—the unemployed, the "welfare takers," the disabled, the homeless. Society looks down on these people because they are not currently generating profit.

Success in the Western, industrialized world is about money, and money is about winning. We must win. Second is for losers, and winning is where the money's at. But why do we bow to success like this? Success does strange things to us. We spend much of our lives in pursuit of it so we can feel good about ourselves and so others will respect us. We put unreal expectations and burdens on our children and push them, filling their lives with busyness so that they can learn the tools to be successful in the world. Because our greatest fear for our kids is not that they will grow up not loving Jesus or out of relationship with us. Our greatest fear for our kids is that they will not be successful.

Valuing success is valuing the wrong thing. Valuing success divides people into the makers and the takers. Valuing success devalues the divine image in a person and replaces it with the divine profit in a person. Valuing success pushes us to raise products instead of raising children. Valuing success puts churches into two categories: growing or dying. And since when did God start valuing success? When the industrialized West started speaking for God.

When Jesus spoke for God, things looked a lot different. Jesus seemed to have placed little value on outward success. Standing in front of a group of people who had been marginalized and oppressed for generations, he said, "Blessed are you who are poor, for yours is the kingdom of God. Blessed are you who hunger now, for you will be satisfied. Blessed are you who weep now, for you will laugh. Blessed are you when people hate you, when they exclude you and insult you and reject your name as evil, because of the Son of Man" (Luke 6:20–22). So Jesus seems to have been saying that if you are poor, hungry, weeping, insulted, and left out, then you are blessed. And blessed seems to be the goal we are going for, right?

But Jesus didn't stop there. He continued: "But woe to you who are rich, for you have already received your comfort. Woe to you who are well fed now, for you will go hungry. Woe to you who laugh now, for you will mourn and weep. Woe to you when everyone speaks well of you, for that is how their ancestors treated the false prophets" (Luke 6:24–26).

We want our systems of success more than we want the blessing of God. People say that money and power are blessings of God. Well, it certainly doesn't look like it here. This all makes sense if you just think about it. This kingdom Jesus was bringing would change everything, and the poor, oppressed, marginalized outcasts were the ones who were going to benefit the most. If the Year of Jubilee was being ushered in and debts were going to be wiped out, then it was indeed those who were indebted who were going to sing and shout in the streets. The rich were going to lose something in this exchange. They would have to forgive the debts; they would have to make room in their systems of power for those who had been excluded.

When Jesus came, the poor and hungry rejoiced because their King had come. And what did the powerful do? They killed him. Because they wanted to keep their power. They wanted to keep their money. They wanted to keep their systems of oppression in place because they made more money when people were oppressed.

When we value success over the image of God in people, then oppression is the most likely outcome. The unchallenged pursuit of success breeds fear and division and creates in us a mind-set that we simply have no use for the coming of the Jubilee of Jesus.

OBEDIENCE

There are not many stories of success in this book, not many stories that make us feel good. The truth is, in our work, there just aren't many remarkable stories of success. Much of what we do is hard. Systems are very difficult to change. People relocate and build relationships with their neighbors only to find their neighbors move six months later. We spend our energy and time tutoring and mentoring kids only to find them leave the church when they are teenagers. This is hard work. I'd like to be able to feed into your desire for success, to feed into my desire for success, but most of the time I just can't.

There are stories of transformation in people's lives. Absolutely. But you will need to see those for yourself. I have no desire to give you a false sense that you are going to save people's lives. You are going to die to yourself and to your desire for paternalistic success stories.

People ask me all the time, "What does success look like in urban ministry?" I've never quite been able to answer this question, and I've just come to realize that the reason I can't answer is because it's the wrong question. One cannot answer it at all.

Mother Teresa reportedly said, "We are not called to success, but to obedience." There it is—obedience is our calling. Not success, but faithfulness. That's why this book is not about success stories, but about the stories and the theology of obedience. People hearing the cry of the oppressed and being obedient to God to engage that pain and brokenness. That's what the parable of the good Samaritan is all about: obedience. That's what urban ministry is about.

Will people be obedient to the message of Jesus to engage the hurting, poor, suffering people of our world? Will we be obedient to love our neighbor? If so, we are called to engage, relocate, and touch. We are not called to fix or to be successful, only to obedience.

Maybe we aren't all called to move into the city, but we are called to care for the poor and oppressed. And to be obedient to that calling in the least, we will have to engage our cities. Today, how can you be obedient to what God is calling you to do?

ASYLUMS

There is this scene in Dostoyevsky's novel, *The Idiot*, where the main character encounters the painting by Hans Holbein called *The Dead Christ in the Tomb*. This is a haunting painting, not something you want to dwell upon. It is exactly what it is called—a depiction of Jesus' corpse before the resurrection.

Dostoyevsky's whole novel was inspired by this painting. Records show that he was both haunted and inspired by this painting in real life. That's what good art will do to you; it will paint a picture of another world. It just looks so real. We don't usually dwell on the dead Christ. We like paintings of Jesus with a sheep on his shoulders or kids playing on his knee. But a painting of the dead Christ in the tomb? That's too real. That hits too close to home.

Maybe we need to be reminded that Jesus did really die and stayed dead for three days. Resurrection is only possible if Jesus was really dead, not pretending to be dead, but really and truly dead. To be people of resurrection, we also need to be people who are not afraid of death.

The Idiot has stuck with me in ways I never expected. To me, the whole book is centered on this idea of resurrection. If Jesus truly was resurrected, which Dostoyevsky and I would agree is indeed the case, then everything should be different. We should live differently and act differently and treat each other differently. Because of the resurrection, we should not be living for ourselves or squabbling in society to see who can get to the top by stepping on as many as possible in order to get there. We should not be mistreating or judging others. We should indeed be pouring out our lives, as our Lord did. Living for something more. Living to show the love of the Resurrected One.

The reality is that so few of us live this way. So few of us see the world this way. The world to us is a game of Monopoly—get as much as you can and destroy everyone else who stands in your way. There is only one winner. Make sure you are it. We are consumed with success but have little attention for obedience.

If we lived out the resurrection, we would seek justice for the oppressed. We would put off the cares and desires of the world and redistribute what we have and who we are for the benefit of others. We would seek to proclaim the love of this resurrected pursuer to all we could in both word and deed. We would, in short, live in agapism.

But then the world would look at us strangely. We wouldn't fit in. We would see love when others see greed. We would see hope when others see doom. We would see precious children of God when others see the color of their skin.

Dostoyevsky concluded his thought on this idea by inferring that if we truly lived like we believed the resurrection, if we lived like lovers of people, as followers of the resurrected Jesus, we, like his hero, would be labeled as idiots. Mentally unstable. Out of touch with reality. The only place for such people is the asylum. If this is indeed the case, then maybe our churches need to look more like asylums of the obedient rather than department stores for the successful.

10 TOUCH

When I was nine, my parents divorced. Even though I was young, I remember this time very clearly. I remember the fights, the throwing of dishes, the slammed doors, the yelling, and the tears that led up to the split. When the marriage was all but lost, my mom, sister, and I moved from North Carolina to Virginia to live with my grandparents. Not only did I lose my father in many ways, I moved to an unfamiliar place and had to make new friends at a new school. I witnessed the intense emotions of a divorce, the tears of my mother, the anger of my father, the crying of my sister, and the uncertainty of our future. For children, the stability of their parents' relationship is critical in emotional development and developing a sense of security in their most foundational relationships. Looking back, I can see that this divorce caused great stress in my life. I can remember crying, being sad and very angry for quite a long time.

Most adults at the time gave me a pass. "The kid has been through a lot," they would say. I was angry with my teachers at school and would frequently get into trouble. I was angry with my grandparents and would fight with them often as well. I was angry with my sister (which may have just been normal), and I was angry with my mother. People were patient with me. They must have understood the stress in my life at this tragic event. My teachers had a great amount of patience with me and somehow understood that I was a smart kid who had potential despite the attitude problems. My grandparents and my mother were also patient with me. Many of those around me were trying to comfort me and deal with my outbursts with grace.

When a kid goes through a traumatic experience, such as seeing loved ones suffer, losing a parent, changing environments, or losing friends, it changes how the child interacts with the world around him or her. It leaves a mark. A mark that needs healing.

When my son was two, my wife and I went to a weeklong conference and left him with his Russian grandparents. He had a great time while we were gone, but when we returned, we were surprised by his reaction to us. We missed him terribly, and we wanted him to run into our arms and give us big hugs to show us how much he missed us. *We* needed to be comforted from our time away. We received a very different reaction.

For the next few days, our son behaved terribly. He hit us, bit us, and lashed out at us in ways he never had before. He got into lots of things he shouldn't have and defied us seemingly on purpose. We didn't understand what was going on. Did one week with the grandparents ruin our kid?

We asked an older, wiser couple who had been through the parenting process many times what they thought of this, and they knew right away. They told us that our child missed us terribly, in a very deep way, and when we returned, this caused strong emotions in him that he simply did not know how to express. He was happy to see us, but because he didn't know how to express the emotions of detachment and then reunion, he lashed out. This was all he knew how to do. His lashing out was saying, "I missed you! Why did you leave? I'm glad to be with you again."

Kids do not express their emotions in the same way adults do. They are in the process of learning how to share their feelings and pain. In an article on children and stress, Dr. Novella Ruffin says, "Children often cannot tell us what they feel or they do not have the language to describe the stressful situation. They tend to show the stress through their behavior. When you notice a three-year-old child crying constantly (or more than usual), or an eight-year-old having a temper tantrum, that may be the child's way of alerting you to something or letting you know that too much is happening."[1]

Kids do not know how to share these emotions, so sometimes we mistake their expressions of emotions as rebellion or hate. The older, wiser parents told us to spend lots of time with our son, hold him and touch him, help him to understand that we were back and that we cared for him. They told us to just be patient with him and love him like crazy, to try not to react to his behavior, read him some stories, and in a few days he would be back to normal. Indeed, in a few days he was back to normal. He just needed a little healing inside. Our absence had caused stress, and that stress needed to be eased by our presence and our care.

PARALYZED

The Gospels give us many accounts of people who encountered Jesus when they needed healing. In fact, there are so many stories of healing that healing seems to be a central aspect of Jesus' ministry. Sometimes, as Western-scientific thinkers, we may be tempted to think that healing is only physical recovery; but this is a mistaken view of the world. As Western people, we have an inherent dualism between the body and spirit, between the physical, spiritual, and emotional, so we have a hard time seeing healing as anything but a physical event.

More and more research is showing that stress makes us ill and can lead to all sorts of physical problems in our bodies. Stress at work, at home, and in our environment, and stress of loss or fear cause sickness. When we are not whole, we are stressed. When we are not whole, we need healing.

Jesus' healings were more than physical events; they were healings of the whole system of the human being: emotional, spiritual, psychological, and physical. To limit his healings to only the physical is to miss the underlying message of the gospel writers, that Jesus is healing every broken system of the cosmos.

There's a story in Mark that highlights this healing of something deeper:

> A few days later, when Jesus again entered Capernaum, the people heard that he had come home. They gathered in such large numbers that there was no room left, not even

> outside the door, and he preached the word to them. Some men came, bringing to him a paralyzed man, carried by four of them. Since they could not get him to Jesus because of the crowd, they made an opening in the roof above Jesus by digging through it and then lowered the mat the man was lying on. When Jesus saw their faith, he said to the paralyzed man, "Son, your sins are forgiven." (Mark 2:1–5)

Why would Jesus say to a paralyzed man, "Your sins are forgiven"? These words seem all wrong and out of place. Jesus seems to be missing the point here. Or maybe *we* are missing the point here. Maybe the real suffering of this man was not his physical ailment, but his spiritual, emotional, psychological ailment. Maybe the deeper issue was the real issue. Maybe his internal stress was affecting his external body. Maybe his internal brokenness was making his body broken.

As we read the Gospels we must always remember that the people of Israel were an oppressed people. The Romans dominated their lives in every single way. The Romans controlled the economy and demanded the people of Israel pay taxes that were unreasonable and unsustainable. People would have to make difficult choices about how they were going to live: Do we pay our taxes, or do we feed our kids? Roman soldiers roamed the streets, reminding everyone who was in charge. They were living in occupied territory. It was their land, but the Romans stole it and forced them to work it. They were enslaved. This is why they wanted rebellion so badly. This is why the "messiah" for them was an expectation of a political deliverer. The oppression they were living under was ruining their lives.[2]

The whole nation was paralyzed with fear and worry. God's people, the people who had been given the God-centered purpose, were living as slaves. But not as slaves to the Romans. Rather, they were living as slaves to their worry and doubt. And they could not move. They could not function. They could not live out God's purpose for their lives because they were paralyzed.

Jesus here was speaking to the real issue, the issue of living under the heavy burden of your failures, worries, brokenness, and stress. Jesus was saying to the man lying on the mat, "Your sins are forgiven. Your past will no longer be held against you. You do not have to live in fear or worry. You do not have to live in separation from God any longer. Receive the healing, and be reunited with your God."

The accumulation of our fears, worries, doubts, and failures is a heavy burden to live under. So heavy, in fact, that we might not be able to move underneath it. It is paralyzing.

Jesus has come to heal us of our past wounds, to set us free from the worry about tomorrow, to make our lives new in every way, to say to our guilt and doubt, "Get out," to say to our fears and worries, "Leave." Jesus understood what the real issue was.

Some of us may look at this and say that Jesus was making sure the man got to heaven by forgiving him his sins. I'm pretty sure that heaven, or the life to come, was not on any of their minds at that moment. This was convincingly about the right now.

We need a healing that goes deep into the depths of our souls, into the halls of our pasts, into the closets of our anxieties. I believe that Jesus is the only one who can offer us this healing.

The story goes on:

> Now some teachers of the law were sitting there, thinking to themselves, "Why does this fellow talk like that? He's blaspheming! Who can forgive sins but God alone?" Immediately Jesus knew in his spirit that this was what they were thinking in their hearts, and he said to them, "Why are you thinking these things? Which is easier: to say to this paralyzed man, 'Your sins are forgiven,' or to say, 'Get up, take your mat and walk'? But I want you to know that the Son of Man has authority on earth to forgive sins." So he said to the man, "I tell you, get up, take your mat and go home." He got up, took his mat and walked out in full view of them all. This amazed everyone and they praised God, saying, "We have never seen anything like this!" (Mark 2:6–12)

"Get up, take up your mat and go home." Jesus was telling the man, "You no longer have to live in exile. You can go home now. You've been living in this wasteland life for so long, cut off from those around you, cut off from God, cut off from even your true self. You've been living as a slave in the foreign land of regret and anxiety. No more. Get up! Take your mat and go home. God is waiting for you. The table is set, and you are the guest of honor. Get out of your exiled land and go home."

Home is where everything makes sense. Home is where people who love you the most are. Home is where God is.

So many of us have been living paralyzed in exile. Jesus is healing the deepest parts of ourselves and setting us free from the bondage of exile. But maybe we as the church have been trying to fix people's outside situation without addressing the accumulation of burdens from their past. We are trying to tell people to get up without first paying attention to their broken souls.

Poverty is not the lack of money; it's the lack of hope. The lack of faith that tomorrow can be any better than today. Poverty is broken dreams. Poverty is broken futures. Poverty is broken hope. And it leaves people paralyzed.

WAR ZONES

Have you ever watched someone close to you go to prison? Have you ever watched or known a family member or close friend be murdered? Have you ever had to worry about where your next meal is going to come from? Have you moved to a new house on average every six months to a year? Most years, did you go to a different school than you did the previous year?

If you live in an urban under-resourced neighborhood then most of your answers will probably be yes. If you live outside an urban under-resourced community (in the suburbs or country or hip-urban), then most of your answers will probably be no.

Here's my point: Life in an under-resourced urban community is very different from life in other places. Not worse or better—

but different. This is something we need to realize as we move forward.

I grew up in the country. I rode my bike all over town in the summer. I walked to the pool and to the gas station to get a candy bar. My friends and I ran all around the neighborhood all day long until our moms called us in for dinner. Nobody ever worried where anyone was. I never knew anyone who was killed. I never even heard stories of someone going to prison. I didn't know what drugs were. I grew up in a very different world than most of our urban children are growing up in.

Growing up in the central city is very hard. Jobs are scarce, and if you don't currently have a job, then finding one is nearly impossible. This means you will most likely have to live off of handouts from someone else. (Please let me assure you, no matter what your perceptions may be, very few people enjoy living off of handouts.) Grocery stores are few and far between, so real food is hard to find, which means you will probably be malnourished. Money is tight, so that might mean you won't eat every night. Chances are that if you grow up in the city someone close to you will be murdered. Chances are even better that someone close to you will go to prison.[3] Drug dealers are on your streets, so you have to watch out. You live in a world of scarcity and limited resources, so everyone is a threat to your existence. You have to be strong, aggressive, and tough. You have to look out for yourself, because everyone around you is a potential threat.

Because of the extreme hardness and difficulty of the life around them, neglect, abuse, and violence are an everyday part of many kids' lives. These factors create great amounts of stress in the lives of urban children. Unbelievable amounts of stress. Levels of stress that can only be compared to stress levels found in war zones.

This is not the children's fault. Neither is it their parents' fault. It is just how life is when you live in a community that is neglected and abandoned.

Why don't we show care to the kids in our cities who are under more stress than the CEO of a major corporation? We don't give these kids a break. Rather, we call them violent. We label them systematic failures. We give up on them at the first sign of trouble. To the world around them and to many of us, they are simply worthless. Why? Because somehow we look at them and expect them to deal with the colossal stresses they are under on a daily basis to simply survive, and we expect them to act like kids.

A few years ago, the CDC released a new study on stresses on children called the ACE study. ACE stands for Adverse Childhood Experiences, and the study measures the amount of stress that children suffer from adverse childhood experiences. Some factors that drive up that amount of stress in children include divorce, neglect, abuse, changing environments, malnutrition, surrounding violence, uncertainty about the future, proximity to crime and substance abuse, domestic violence, and more. The ACE study reveals that the more of these adverse experiences children encounter, the more stress is placed on their lives, and therefore the more likely the children are to express these stresses in violence of their own or in the form of substance abuse.[4]

Our kids in our cities are not lashing out because they are violent; they are lashing out because they are suffering. They are not suffering because they are in poverty; they are in poverty because they are suffering. Their world has been destroyed before their very eyes. By the time they are teenagers, hope has all but faded from their view. They are suffering deeply.

I often heard people say, "Well, they just need to get an education." Let me ask you this: How well does your kid do in school when he or she experiences stress at home? Stress at home is a leading cause of problems at school. In fact, because the stresses of living in these environments are so heavy upon kids, they actually produce what scientists call "emotional dysregulation," a state that makes learning almost impossible.

Kids can't learn with all of these environmental stressors. It doesn't matter how good the education system is. Kids simply cannot learn when every piece of their lives is falling apart around them every day.

The ACE study shows us that adverse childhood experiences lead to social, emotional, and cognitive impairments, which lead to adoption of health-risk behaviors, which lead to disease, disability, and social problems, which invariably will lead to an early death.

In other words, when you experience these stressors as a child, they don't just go away; you carry them with you into adulthood. They begin to rule your life, leaving you paralyzed.

Throwing money at our cities won't help. Trying to fix our city schools by adding security or new textbooks or more tests won't help. Granted, focusing money and educational improvements is needed and beneficial, but the fact remains that there is something much deeper going on here. Our cities are suffering under generations of brokenness, racism, isolation, unemployment (often due to lack of available jobs), drugs, and disenfranchisement. They need healing. Our cities need healing at a deep level—at the deep level only Jesus can offer. But to be part of that healing process, we are going to have to get close. We are going to have to change our proximity.

In the midst of this despair, there is hope, and there can be healing. The scientific answer that more and more are gravitating to is called "trauma-informed care."[5] The foundation for this type of care is the initial perspective. This is care that changes the perspective from "What is wrong with you?" to "What happened to you?" It is care that changes the perspective from treating the outward response of the deep trauma and stress to the deep brokenness due to the trauma and stress.

It changes everything.

Dr. Howard Bath, the Children's Commissioner of the Northern Australian Territories, wrote a paper on trauma-informed care called "The Three Pillars of Trauma-Informed Care."[6] In it, he outlined the three pillars that are essential to the process of healing in children suffering under the great stress of adverse experiences: First, create a safe space for the child, a place where the child feels comfortable and safe from danger or violence; second, build comfortable connections between the child and caring adults; third, help the child manage emotions and impulses. Have those caring adults in safe places actively listen to the child when his or her emotions run wild. Seek to co-regulate and give names to negative emotions in order to help the child understand the positive and negative ways of reacting to internal stressors.

Essentially, this is love. The kind of love we gave to our two-year-old when he lashed out at us. The kind of love that cares enough for a person to see past behavior to the deep need, that is willing to wade through the muck and mire of layers of desperation to see the image of God that was there all along. The kind of love that is not satisfied with throwing pity or charity at the problem, but is willing to get involved.

It is loving enough to not label. It is loving enough to not stay away. It is loving enough to get close. This is what we are called to do, church—to get close. To change our proximity. Everything depends on this simple act of relocation.

When the paralyzed man was brought to Jesus, Jesus knew what the man needed. The man needed healing deep in his soul. So do our cities. They have been under the oppression of evil forces for generations, and our calling is to engage, to look deeply at our cities, and say, "You bear the image of God, and he wants to heal you—to heal your past, your future, and your present. You are valuable and worthy. We love you, and God loves you."

The kids in our cities need us, but we need them too. We need them as much as they need us. We need their experiences, their sufferings, their potential to impact our lives as well. We are not whole without each other. God is a God of unity, and neither we nor they can experience this deep healing unless we see that we both need each other equally.

We are all broken people, every one of us. We all need the healing Jesus offers. We are not going to find that unless we realize we are not whole—that we need the experiences, the wisdom, and the suffering of our cities. We need to leave behind the attitude that we are coming to be the blessers and realize that we are coming to *be* blessed. The hurting kids who grow up to be hurting adults hold the blessing for our lives. Yes, I know this makes little sense on the surface, and it's hard to explain, but it's the truth.

Jesus is saying to us all, "Your sins are forgiven." The power of your past is broken because of the power of Christ. So get up! Pick up your mat and go home. No, I'm not talking to the city—I'm talking to you. Don't be paralyzed by the accumulation of your fear toward the city; get up and go home. Jesus is setting you free to join in with the pain and suffering of others. Don't isolate yourself in your prisons of picket fences and two-car garages. Be reconciled to those you don't understand. Be reconciled to those you have looked down upon for so long. For many people, the key to healing, to wholeness, lies in the city.

Go, and you may just realize that you were the one who needed healing in the first place.

TABLE FELLOWSHIP

There's something powerful in eating meals together, isn't there? Within every ministry at our church, we always plan and organize regular meals. When these meals occur, there is no teaching, no study, just sitting and eating together. Sharing a meal brings people together. It builds trust and opens hearts. Often, it begins the process of reconciliation between those sitting together.

Reconciliation is the process of putting things back the way they were intended to be. When a married couple goes through separation but finds reconciliation, they find forgiveness for one another and come back together again to live and relate to one another in covenant once more. When friends fall out but find forgiveness and understanding and come together in grace and harmony, they find reconciliation.

To reconcile, forgiveness must take place, debts must be lifted, barriers must be broken down, and the covenant of mutual love must be reestablished. Reconciliation is central to the message of Scripture—with God, with others, and with ourselves. Paul said it this way:

> So from now on we regard no one from a worldly point of view. Though we once regarded Christ in this way, we do so no longer. Therefore, if anyone is in Christ, the new creation has come: The old has gone, the new is here! All this is from God, who reconciled us to himself through Christ and gave us the ministry of reconciliation: that God was reconciling the world to himself in Christ, not counting people's sins against them. And he has committed to us the message of reconciliation. We are therefore Christ's ambassadors, as though God were making his appeal through us. (2 Cor. 5:16–20)

Some scholars have said that this message of reconciliation was the central message of Paul's teaching to the young churches of his day. You may agree when we are talking about reconciliation with God—to be restored in relationship with God. But how is it possible to be reconciled to God and not to our neighbor? If we are ambassadors, God's representatives to humanity, then shouldn't we be reconciled with one another?

The situation in the early church that Paul was addressing in these letters was not unlike our own in many respects. Within these early communities of Jesus followers, there was a great dilemma of division, and one of the central questions was simply, "How will we relate to one another here?"

In Roman society, there was great division among classes of people. There were divisions of race between Jews and Gentiles, of economics between rich and poor, of gender between men and women, and of status between slaves and free people. In Roman society, a rich, free man had no need to be in relationship with a woman, slave, or Jew. In fact, it went further than this. A rich, free man could not even mingle with people of a lower social class as equals. Rich, free, Roman men would see it as their right to oppress and use people in lower social classes. Rich, free, Roman men would see it as their right to sexually abuse women in lower social classes.

But the revolutionary message of the early church community was this: As followers of Jesus, "there is neither Jew nor Gentile, neither slave nor free, nor is there male and female, for you are all one in Christ Jesus" (Gal. 3:28).

That posed major problems. This had implications that would move beyond the moments of church fellowship. In this place, at Communion, all of these parties would eat a meal together, and in so doing they would be saying to everyone at the table that they were now equals. At this table, there was no one above and no one below. At this table, there was no slave and no slave-owner. At this table, there would be no oppression or pain. At this table, they were brothers and sisters, and they were all responsible for one another.

And a message I believe Paul was driving home was that now, in Christ, you do not regard one another from the old worldly point of view of class and race and economics, but you have all been made new, and so go, now, outside these walls and live outside like you live inside: free of oppression.

This was hard. But this was the message of reconciliation. This was the ministry of reconciliation that they were being called ambassadors for.

In the opening chapters of Mark, Jesus also established this message of reconciliation with table fellowship. The religious leaders didn't like this very much. Reconciliation is offensive.

> Once again Jesus went out beside the lake. A large crowd came to him, and he began to teach them. As he walked along, he saw Levi son of Alphaeus sitting at the tax collector's booth. "Follow me," Jesus told him, and Levi got up and followed him. While Jesus was having dinner at Levi's house, many tax collectors and sinners were eating with him

> and his disciples, for there were many who followed him. When the teachers of the law who were Pharisees saw him eating with the sinners and tax collectors, they asked his disciples: "Why does he eat with tax collectors and sinners?" (Mark 2:13–16)

In the opening of his gospel, Mark made it abundantly clear that Jesus brought together people who were previously cut off from one another. Until now, his disciples had been fishermen. Fishermen did not like tax collectors; nobody did, for that matter. And who did Jesus bring into his close-knit group of disciples? Sure enough—a tax collector.

What is going on here? This quote from *The Eucharistic Words of Jesus* may shed some light on this for us: "For the Israelite, every table fellowship is a guarantee of peace, trust, or brotherhood. . . . They, to whom symbolic action means more than it does for us, would immediately understand the acceptance of the outcasts into table fellowship with Jesus as an offer of salvation to the guilty sinners and as the assurance of forgiveness. Hence the objections of the Pharisees . . . who held that the pious could only have table fellowship with the righteous."[7]

This was not simply a meal; this was a statement. In the Jewish culture, when two people shared a meal together, that meant they were being reconciled, any debts that had accumulated between the parties were being forgiven, and if there was any reason for one party to be excluded or cut off from society because of their debts, well, that was being done away with.

Why would the religious leaders be upset about this? Why would they care? Because Jesus, here, as in the rest of the early chapters of Mark, was forgiving those who were held under a huge debt. Sinners were those who owed something to someone. Sinners were outcasts. Sinners were the lowest of society. And Jesus was eating with them. Jesus was declaring that they were equals. Jesus was declaring that they were forgiven. Jesus was declaring that he was in relationship with them as brothers and sisters.

The "righteous" religious leaders did not like this at all. Why? Because they were the ones who had something to lose. If the debts of these "sinners" were being forgiven, the rigid social boundaries that the religious leaders had created to sustain their superiority and prestige were being broken down.

The Pharisees called these people *sinners*, a derogatory word, loaded with meaning. You were a sinner because you owed someone something. You were a sinner because you were outside of God's blessing on your life. You were a sinner because there was something wrong with you, some disability or some illness. It's not like the way we use the term today. But we do the same things as the Pharisees, don't we? We put people down, blame them for something that is not their fault, put ourselves above them for no apparent reason but our race, gender, or socioeconomics. I wonder who Jesus would be eating with today if he were here.

Notice what Jesus said later on: "It is not the healthy who need a doctor, but the sick. I have not come to call the righteous, but sinners" (Mark 2:17). Jesus was being ironic in using the terms *righteous* and *sinners* together, seemingly flipping their value, but he did something else we should pay attention to. He called the people he was eating with "sick." Not in a negative way; I think he was referring to them for what they were—broken, isolated, and hurting. They were sick because they had been cut off from society. They were sick because of the oppression and isolation they were living under. They were sick not because of what they had done, but because of what had happened to them.

Jesus was dining with them, getting close, providing a safe place of love and grace, and inviting the question, "What happened here?" He was entering into the deep societal brokenness and division as the ambassador of reconciliation. And it all took place at a table with some food.

This is why the ACE study on trauma-informed care is so interesting—because Jesus knew it long before anyone did a study on it and labeled it "scientific." Jesus got close to the pain. He understood that God's people were hurting and dying under the pressure of the divisions and hatred of society, so he entered into this situation and dined with it.

If you think we don't need reconciliation today, think again. If you don't think there are deep prejudices in our race relations and our economic classes, think again. It's a difficult message, but it's central to the message of Scripture, and we must be willing to enter into this conversation. We must be willing to dine with those who are different from us, who have different-colored skin than ours, who live in different places than us, and work at different jobs than us.

GO HOME

If you don't see the Scriptures leading us to engage our cities and one another and if you don't believe our experiences with urban ministry, then listen to the science. Scientists are backing up what we are doing, what followers of Jesus have been doing for generations. In order to bring healing to our cities, or wherever there is poverty and brokenness, you are needed—your presence, your life, your touch. In order to have table fellowship, you have to get close, to touch, to put yourself right in the middle of it all. Science is telling us we need to change our proximity. We have to get closer. We can't care for the suffering at a distance. We have to get close enough to touch lives on an everyday basis. To offer trauma-informed care, we have to be close, not far.

Just like the paralyzed man who was brought to Jesus, we cannot pull anyone out of poverty. Poverty is deeper than that and must be dealt with from within. Many of us live in the pits of poverty. Even some of us who are very rich are still so very poor and broken. To engage poverty, we have to engage suffering. This is what Jesus was doing over and over again, because that's where healing begins.

One cannot be simply pulled out of this state of deep suffering. One must be healed from within. One must be forgiven and receive the forgiveness that goes deep and changes everything. Not just a spiritual forgiveness, but a very physical and relational forgiveness as well—the type of forgiveness that heals our wounded souls and allows us to pick up our mats and go home.

That means we have to get close and stay close to one another. We can't be revolving doors, coming and going. Safe places will never be created if we are constantly leaving, retreating to our own citadels of comfort. We have to establish these places of refuge in the city, among the people. We can't ever build trust if we are constantly leaving. We have to stay; we have to listen; we have to touch; we have to dine, hug, care for, and sacrifice for; and we have to endure outbursts and understand that these outbursts only reveal the deep pain.

We have to change our perceptions. We have to see people, not as society has labeled them, but as God sees them—beautiful and magnificent humans. We have to change our perception from seeing people as having nothing to offer to seeing them as having much to offer.

People living in our cities have suffered greatly and have learned from their experiences. Maybe we need to learn from them how to suffer well, how to hold to God in the midst of persecution. Maybe we need to learn from them how to survive and thrive when resources are limited, learn ingenuity, sharing, and endurance. Suburban America would do well to listen to the accumulated wisdom of those living in our cities.

When my son was stressed, he reacted violently toward us, so we held him, played with him, stayed near him, read him stories, and constantly reminded him in both words and deeds that we love him and will never leave him.

This is what all of us need, no matter where we live or our race or gender. We all need healing; we all need to listen and learn from one another; we all need forgiveness. And the only way we are going to find that is with one another. Sitting at the table, touching one another, listening to one another, seeing the God-spark within each of us, sharing our stories and experiences, and asking each other, "What happened? Why are we all so divided and full of pain?" That is the only thing that will heal the past wounds, the past sins, the past pains of both us and them . . . whoever "us" and "them" really are. This is the only thing that will bring reconciliation. Let's be the ambassadors of hope we were called to be.

11

THE LAST CHAPTER PART 1

STORY

It has become popular to split the last chapter into two parts, so I thought I'd do the same.

As a missions-minded person, I was trained to look at how the gospel interacts with other cultures. The tricky thing about culture is that it's hard to see. No, let me be more specific. It's not hard to see someone else's culture; it's hard to see our own culture. Culture is something we grow up in, like the air around us. It is not something we think about or evaluate. It simply is. But once we begin to look at other cultures, then we can begin to look at our own.

It is hard for Western Christians to see the influence of the culture of individualism on their faith. It is hard for Americans to see the influence of nationalism on the church. But it is there.

As we look at how the gospel interacts with cultures around the world, we often see how the church is persecuted in other parts of the world. How the Soviets put down the church. How the Chinese oppress Christianity. On and on we could go.

Something that I have often heard when people pray aloud, or in conversation, and probably said myself, is this: "Thank you, Lord, that we can live in a land where the church is not persecuted . . . a land in which we can gather freely and without danger."

I'm thankful that we can live in a land where we can worship freely. It is remarkable and a testimony to the laws of our land. But as I look at other cultures in the world, and throughout history, I see that, although persecution is a terrible thing, the church often thrives in it. Persecution solidifies us. It gives us a meaning behind our worship and our gathering. Quite honestly, I wish there was a little more persecution of the church in America, because persecution helps to refine us, like fire, and I think we would all agree that we need some refining.

In the process of writing this book and trying to examine my own American-Western culture, I think I am changing my tune about this whole thing. We believe there is no persecution of the church in America, but I'm beginning to see things differently. Yes, no one is putting us in prison for worshiping Jesus. We still get our tax exemptions and tax breaks for being a church. We can form churches and worship in them quite freely. But there's something deeper going on. Something more devious. Our enemy is pretty crafty.

In a classic line in the movie *The Usual Suspects*, Kevin Spacey's character speaks of "the devil" by saying, "The greatest trick the devil ever pulled was convincing the world he doesn't exist."[1] This is true on so many levels.

Another great trick is making us believe we are not being persecuted. The persecution of the American church is not a frontal attack, but rather it's convincing us to live by another philosophy, to give our souls to something other than Jesus. And so many of us are falling for it.

Look at the culture we have embraced as a church: We want to be individuals, but Scripture talks about true community. We want more stuff, but we are called to simplicity and giving things away. We are infused with greed, but a central idea in Paul's letters is radical generosity. We so anxiously chase after safety, but we are left with a calling of risk. We worship celebrity when self-denial is our standard. We pity when we should love. We comply with injustice when we should stand for justice. We embrace a culture of violence when our lives should be symbols of peace. We live for the kingdom of America when we are called to live for the kingdom of God.

The persecution has not come from the front. It has disguised itself in such a way that we do not even realize it exists. But the reality is that so many values we hold dear as followers of Jesus, so many values that Scripture has taught us to live by, are being eroded by the culture around us, which we so seldom see. We are being persecuted, not by our government, but rather by our own culture.

Paul said, "Do not conform to the pattern of this world, but be transformed by the renewing of your mind. Then you will be able to test and approve what God's will is—his good, pleasing and perfect will" (Rom. 12:2). "World" here is another word for culture. "Renewing of your mind" is another way of saying "change your mind." Change your mind, change your life.

People often ask me, "How do I know the will of God for my life?" I tell them, "Go serve others and you will see it." We have a hard time seeing, testing, or approving God's will because we have conformed to our culture. The church looks more like America than like Jesus. This is a problem. We need to change our minds. We need to live by a different message. Not the message of our culture, but the message of Scripture. We need to live by a different story.

STORY-FORMED COMMUNITY

We all love a good story—whether it is played out in a novel, in a movie, on TV, or even in our own lives. Good stories are powerful and shape our lives. How often have you heard the story of how God moved in a person's life in an amazing way and been blessed, encouraged, inspired, and reassured that God is still moving? How often have your read or seen a good story and it inspires you to change something in your life? Or to treat your loved ones better? Or to give up a habit? Or to pursue another career?

Stories matter. They define us; they inspire us; they change us. We can't change our minds without having a story to help transform us. This is why the message of Scripture comes in a series of stories. It's not just a list of dos and don'ts or facts and data.

The story of humanity and the story of God in pursuit of this humanity and this pursuit culminating in the life, teachings, message, and radical resistance of Jesus is something to inspire the world.

There is simply no way around it: We are a story people. And we are a story-formed community. The stories of those who have gone before us inspire and propel us. The stories of how the great saints, "the cloud of witnesses," have followed Jesus in crazy ways show us God's faithfulness and grace. The stories of God's work in the community of Israel, the stories of God becoming man in Jesus, the stories of the early church—we have these accounts of God's grace passed down to us through stories.

These stories form us. They transform us.

But so many of us and so many of our churches are being formed by the wrong story. We are being formed by the story and values of our culture instead of the stories and values of Scripture. These two stories are not the same. They are not compatible.

This whole book has been about the story we are called to live in. You have read about many who have gone before us, about the heroes of our faith, mainly Jesus. These stories have one point: to wake us up! To show us that we are called to live by a different story, not the story of our culture, not the story of greed consumerism, pity, self-interest, violence, individualism, success, and on and on. But we are called to live out the radical story of God's faithfulness to a broken humanity as seen most clearly through the life, message, and resurrection of Jesus.

That story is not safe. That story is not easy. That story is radical. That story is dangerous. Because when we start living out that story, we do not "just go along" with everything around us, with the values of our culture. We become a danger to the culture because our values contradict the world's values.

People will notice, and they will not like it. They will be convicted not by our condemnation, but by the story we are living in, the story that is forming our lives and our every decision and how different that story is from their story.

In his amazing book *Exiles*, Michael Frost speaks directly to this:

> So too with the Jewish exiles in Babylon and the Christian movement today: we are a story-formed community. The Christian experience is not primarily formed by our liturgy, doctrine, or ecclesiology, as important as those might be. We are formed by the dangerous stories of our great hero. Just as the rabbit's instinct is to stop and dig, so too our very human instinct is to embrace safety, warmth, and security. Our all-too-human impulses push us toward being untroubled. We build homes, embrace respectability, and try not to stand out. We want to escape into the cool, cool earth rather than to cut out across the open fields, courting danger, negotiating challenges. So what will get us up and out of our safe warrens? What will continue to foster unease about being exiled in a post-Christendom world? Surely it will be the radical stories of Jesus, the prince with a thousand enemies.[2]

The stories passed down to us in Scripture are dangerous. Moses standing up before Pharaoh and declaring to him, "Let my people go" is a dangerous story. Daniel standing up before the king is a dangerous story. And of course, the most important story of all—Jesus' story—is a dangerous story. Remember, Jesus' murder by the state was engineered by the religious leaders and celebrated among the powerful. Jesus was a danger. The incarnation is dangerous. Justice in the temple is dangerous. The crucifixion is dangerous. The resurrection is dangerous. These are the stories that should be forming us, not the stories of safety and success passed down to us by our culture.

As we reach the climax of this discussion, this is the point of it all: We are called for something bigger, something more than to simply advance the ways and values of the culture around us. We are called to live out the dangerous message of Jesus in the world around us that brings hope, healing, and restoration to the world. We simply cannot stay safe. Living out the way of Jesus will get us in trouble, it will cause us to lose something, it will lead us to put our lives and futures in positions where we could lose something. But we can no longer look at injustice and stay silent. We can no longer follow self-interest as a way of personal happiness. We can no longer propagate division among races or economic levels. We can no longer stand behind the political ideology of blame instead of taking personal responsibility for our neighbor. The story that Jesus has called us into is bigger than all of this. We are a dangerous presence within a dangerous story.

> Recalling the stories of Jesus is one affront to the empire [or culture], but a second cause of annoyance to that

> empire is the resolute commitment by a few stouthearted souls to imagine a shift of power in the world, a shift from greed and self-righteousness to love and justice. The Christian movement must be the living, breathing promise to society that it is possible to live out the values of Christ—that is, to be a radical, troubling alternative to the power imbalances in the empire. In a world of greed and consumerism, the church ought to be a community of generosity and selflessness.[3]

We have been given the stories of dangerous imagination, to believe that something else is possible. The culture around us is saying, "Peace, Peace," but we rise up like the prophet Jeremiah and say, "No! There is no peace here! There is injustice everywhere!" We believe that another world is possible through the power of Christ. Injustice does not have to reign any longer, because our imaginations have been set free from the chains of the status quo in such a way that we can see what redemption and freedom truly look like. Thus we then proceed to turn our dangerous imagination into radical restoration. And to put that dangerous imagination into action we will have to practice dangerous criticism. When there is some human-diminishing activity working in this world, then we, as the church, must take a stand and declare it for what it is—wrong.

There will be consequences for our criticism; that's why it's dangerous. We will be spoken out against; we will lose our prestige. We may even lose our tax-exempt status. But we are the body of the resurrected Jesus, and we are the ones with true power—not them, us. Let us be that dangerous criticism to our leaders; let us unite with one voice and demand change. Let us be like the voice of Amos in our world, declaring, "Let justice roll on like a river, righteousness like a never-failing stream!" (Amos 5:24).

We must be appalled at the loss of life in any way. We must be appalled at the injustice of using people as products or slaves. We must be appalled at poverty. We must be appalled at violence. We must be appalled at division along class or racial lines.

And finally, it is the task of the church to embrace once more our practice of dangerous laments. We sing songs of happiness and wonder in our churches. We pray prayers of thanksgiving and blessing, but where are our songs and prayers of lament? The Psalms are filled with them. "How long will you defend the unjust and show partiality to the wicked? Defend the weak and the fatherless; uphold the cause of the poor and the oppressed. Rescue the weak and the needy; deliver them from the hand of the wicked" (Ps. 82:2–4).

There are so many things that are just not right about the world. Why do we stay quiet about them? We need to regain our ability to lament—to cry out and call wrong wrong. To pray dangerous prayers within our communities to ask God to intervene in the deaths of our innocent.

We have seen so much wrong that we have become jaded to it all. This is why we have embraced violence so fully; we don't even see it anymore. We need to recapture the ability to be surprised.

Chris Rice and Emmanuel Katongole say in their article "A Christian Vision of Reconciliation":

> Praise and lament are the twin sisters of the Psalms, and they are always walking hand-in-hand. To lament is to learn to see, stand in, describe, and tell the truthful story about the brokenness around us and in us. To lament is to learn to refuse to be consoled by easy explanations or false hopes. Lament is bringing our analysis into conversation with God and learning to pray with urgency. Lament is the practice of becoming joined with others into God's desires, a journey into seeing what God sees and feeling what God feels.[4]

They are saying, "Listen everyone. This is not normal. This should not happen. We cannot stand by and just pretend this isn't happening. Look and see, everyone. Look and see. God, we are crying out for you to move. Please hear us!"

This is our task and our message: to boldly proclaim that injustice anywhere is injustice everywhere. Our task is to have the courage to embrace holy indignation. Our calling is to be a dangerous presence in the world. To announce by our words and deeds that there is a better story to live by—a story that will bring hope and resurrection, not despair and death.

If we live by this story and live this life, then we must engage our cities in a greater way. We cannot bury our heads and hearts in the sand. We cannot create our own Christian ghettos of comfort and safety. We cannot turn our eyes to the injustice that is occurring a few miles from our homes.

Yes, I agree there are problems everywhere. Pastors in the suburbs often say to me, "We have as many problems here as you have in the city." This is a false statement. Yes, every town and suburb has broken people and needs redemption. Absolutely. We need passionate churches and leaders in the suburbs and the country teaching their people to live by this dangerous message and to fight injustice in their context too.

But it is simply not on a scale that we see in our cities. Poverty reigns unchecked in our cities. Pimps traffic and exploit with no recourse. Schools are failing. Neighborhoods are falling apart. Kids are growing up with little hope. The American city is a gathering place for injustice. It all gets sent here. It's not the same.

But let's look up, church. There is such beauty here in the city. People come into the city and start complaining about all the problems. But look up and see the beauty! These neighborhoods are beautiful. These people are special and talented. They are beloved by God. These kids are smart and beautiful and deserve better than what they are getting, and oftentimes all they need is a mentor or tutor or just a pair of glasses. Mothers who have sacrificed everything for their kids live here. It's not ugly; it's beautiful. There is deep and connected community within our cities that we need to learn from.

Please, see it for what it's worth. Chances are that your life was broken at one point too. Maybe others looked at you and said, "It's not worth it." But Jesus saw past all that. Jesus saw the reflection of the image of God in you and went to a cross to redeem you from the clutches of evil and oppression.

The city is just as beautiful. It's worth our sacrifices. It's worth our work. If we are going to be formed by this dangerous story, inspired by our dangerous imaginations, and changed by our dangerous laments in order to live as a dangerous presence, then we must go to the places where injustice reigns and cry out with the collective shouts of our lives, "This is wrong and it cannot stand!"

Simply put, if we live this way, I believe it will lead many of us on a journey to our cities because it is uniquely within our cities that injustice and oppression have concentrated to form a fog of pain that only the power of the people of the resurrected Jesus can break. No, we are not Saviors, but we follow in the footsteps of One.

12

THE LAST CHAPTER PART 2

EVERYTHING

As I write this book, I'm teaching a series on the book of Revelation. We tend not to talk about Revelation very much in the church. It's difficult to understand, shrouded in mystery, and uses images and metaphors that we are not accustomed to. Our minds struggle with it on many levels. Because of all this misunderstanding and difficulty, we have done something terrible to Revelation—we have made it all about the future.

Popular Christian culture has tried to tell us that Revelation is all about the future, about another time, another people, other events. Christian pop culture has convinced us that Revelation tells us we will get out of all the trouble and persecution and suffering with the mysterious "rapture."[1]

But Scripture is easy to read when it's never about us. It's easy to handle when it is never about right now. It's easy to talk about when it never speaks to our sin.

Why do you think in America we've turned so much of the Christian faith into a conversation about a time somewhere in the future and a place somewhere far from here? It's easier that way. We don't have to deal with right now when it's all about later.

When we read Revelation as a "Dummy's Guide to the Apocalypse," we miss the whole point. And we miss it badly. This is why it so often doesn't make any sense to us. This is why we don't read it or understand it. This is why we stay away from it.

But this is a mistake.

The book of Revelation is not about later; it is always about right now. No matter what time and place you live in, it's about right here and right now. And when we read it this way, it punches us in the face. And it hurts.

Let me explain. Revelation was written to a group of Christians who were suffering great persecution and uncertainty in the face of the Roman Empire in the first century. Remember, Revelation is first and foremost a letter coming directly from Jesus to the seven churches. In this letter, Jesus reassured these churches that he is in charge of all things. That he is Lord over all creation. That he has all the power. That the future is his. This is what the life-changing vision of Jesus seated upon the throne in Revelation 1 is all about. It's a message of comfort to the early Christians to say to them that he is in charge of all things and no one can defeat him. That Jesus is in charge of the course of history, not Caesar, not Satan.

And his message to his church is this: "Worship me. I'm the Lord of all creation, so worship me and me alone. Don't worship Rome. Don't worship Caesar. Don't worship money or trade. Don't worship your career or your future. Don't worship any of these things. Worship only me."

He told the people that things will be difficult, that they will suffer and some of them will die, but not to lose hope. God is bringing about his preferred future. God will not micromanage the world, but he will never leave it alone.

God told the early Christians they would suffer. We don't like this message much, so we make up our own that takes suffering out of the equation. We make up our own story about God getting us out of suffering and pain with a wave of his magic wand. But that's not God's story. That's the American dream story. And God's story is not America's story.

Revelation points the finger back at us and tells us that we are lukewarm. We are worshiping the empire, money, power, sex, comfort, and security, and we are looking more like the empire than the kingdom of Jesus. Today, does the church look more like America or Jesus? Are we made in America's image or Jesus' image?

Revelation tells us that our calling is to worship Jesus above all things and to live our lives for him . . . no matter what. Jesus was saying to the church, "You might get killed, but that's OK. I'm still in charge, so worship me. Besides, if you worship the empire, you will be dead inside already."

You might not work your way up the corporate ladder; you might have to take a path of downward mobility. That's OK; worship the Lamb on the throne. You might put your family in danger or you might get persecuted or you might not have a lot of money. You might even suffer. That's OK; worship the Lamb on the throne.

Jesus says, "It's OK; worship me."

You see, this is getting dangerous. Revelation is dangerous, so we push it underground. It is hazardous to our well-being because God is telling us that he is not going to get us out of anything. Rather, we are going to have to go through the fire, like Shadrach, Meshach, and Abednego in the furnace, like Daniel in the lion's den.

Our calling is to remain faithful in the midst of suffering and persecution, to worship God always no matter what. Our calling is to be formed in God's image, not another's image—not an idol's image, not money's image, not success's image. Our calling is to live for the kingdom of God, not the kingdom of anything else.

It all gets hard, doesn't it? It all demands too much, doesn't it? We like the other story, the smaller story, the false story that tells us we will get all our desires met, that Santa God will bring us gifts of money, power, success, and security. That's a false story. It's not God's story.

God's story is dangerous.

We read Revelation and think it's about sometime far away, and we so seldom point the finger at ourselves. We look around us and see that the church is struggling around us, the people are abandoning the faith left and right, and we point our finger to the government or to culture or to the youth or homosexuals or taxes or whatever it is. It's not their fault.

You want to know why the church in America is struggling? It's our fault. Mine. Yours. It's the church's fault.

We have been worshiping everything else but Jesus. We have been worshiping our money and allowing it to dictate how we will live our lives. We take the mark of the beast over and over again, and that's the image written on our forehead, not the image of the cross, not the image of the way of Jesus. We worship the American dream and try to get ahead, form our lives, and make decisions on what is best for our career advancement and how successful we can possibly be.

We live for self-satisfaction, in an attempt to have a flourishing life, so we move where we want and go where we want and give little attention to our church community. We serve ourselves, our future, and our desires instead of the kingdom of God. We surround ourselves in layers of security instead of taking risks for Jesus. We insulate ourselves from suffering and build walls to protect us from those who are.

Out of sight, out of mind. If we don't see the suffering, we won't have to feel bad about the suffering, and we certainly won't have to engage it.

And the world can see right through us. We come into our churches and raise our hands and then go live for ourselves. We are pretending to worship Jesus, but in reality, we are worshiping everything else—and the world can see it. It's all too clear to everyone else but us. The world knows that we will be known by our fruits. The world knows that we should be known by our love. They see right through us. They see what we are really about, and they are spitting us out of their mouths. They want nothing to do with a religion that talks about heaven and neglects the world around us that is living in hell. They want nothing to do with a God who talks about love, but then those followers use their neighbors as commodities to be traded. They refuse to follow a God who gave those followers a commission to be ambassadors of reconciliation and who still divide themselves along race, gender, and economics. They see right through us, and they don't want any part of it.

But it is easier this way. I agree. Because if we worship Jesus, then we are surrendering our lives, future, money, time, and talents to him. That means they are his and not ours. That means that our lives should be formed in his image—the image of the One who suffered and died for those he loves. The image of One who refused to allow injustice to flourish. The image of the One who was murdered because he stood against the forces of evil. The image of the One who stayed in Lyahi and ate orange peels with the orphaned children. The image of the One who lives in the 'hood. The image of the One who dines with the outsiders, the marginalized, and the outcasts. The image of the One who emptied himself.

If we surrender our lives and worship the Lamb who was slain, then we are putting our lives and our futures at risk. If we surrender our lives, then that means we are not in control of them anymore. We don't get to dictate where we will go or what we will do; we simply have to follow. Following is risky, because you don't know where the one you follow will lead you.

That's why we make Revelation about the future, not about now. That's why we make Jesus' teachings about the future or about "them," not about right now and certainly not about "us." It is always easier this way. Following Jesus is hard, and it will cost us everything.

This all sounds very difficult, and well, it is. But this message is infused with hope and radical healing of us and our world. We lose so much when we make Revelation or anything else in Scripture exclusively about the future. We lose the capacity of Scripture to speak to us right now. And when we do this, we live under the mistaken theology that hope and healing will only happen in a future, faraway place. No—the kingdom of God means it can happen now! This is the life that Jesus is calling us to live, and if we dare to live it—truly live it—it will transform our lives and the lives around us. We will see our lives begin the process of healing—healing the wounds of idolatry and freeing us from the chains of self-satisfaction and the pursuit of more.

This is the grand paradox of the Christian life. We serve the God of self-denial, and we are called to be the people of self-denial. And this is actually the path that leads to resurrection. When we die to all these other voices in our lives, we are free to live for the voice that truly matters—the voice of the Lamb on the throne of the cosmos.

But a seed cannot grow until it dies. And a life cannot find its purpose until it surrenders control. This is the way of hope. This is the way of healing. This is the way of restoration.

TURNING OVER TABLES

Jesus spent most of his ministry time in the countryside. He was healing, teaching, delivering, and doing amazing things in the countryside. He probably could have stayed in the country and ministered and lived to be an old man. He was not a threat in the country. He could be isolated and managed in the country. But Jesus knew that he must come face-to-face with the centers of power of oppression, and those powers were in Jerusalem—in the city.

Now, don't misunderstand me. I'm not bashing the country. I was raised in the country, and there are amazing people in the country with amazing churches doing amazing things. Jesus is at work in the countryside all around this world, and his followers are doing great things there. We need great ministries and committed followers of Jesus working in the country, in the rural areas, in the suburbs. My point is twofold. First, most people do not fear working in the country or working in the suburbs, but we fear the city. We do not make divisions with the people living in the country or suburbs, but we do the city. The city is different, and it is not a place many want to go work in. Second, the city is the center of culture. Historically, cities have been and still are the centers of philosophy, culture, art, and music. And the city is where the people are. Over 80 percent of our world's population now lives in cities. The cities are vital to the direction of any culture and any movement.

And furthermore, for Jesus the temple was in the city, and there was about to be a showdown. So he rode in on his donkey, declaring to all that the King had arrived.[2] But he didn't stop there. He walked into the temple, the center of Jewish life and pride, the center of politics and philosophy, the center of worship and mission, and he turned over the tables of injustice. He refused to allow the injustices of buying and selling and oppression and exclusion to happen in the place where God was to be worshiped. He refused to sit by while the accumulated weight of social stratification and division robbed people of their future. He refused to be complicit in neglecting the true meaning of the law: love. So he tore down the systems and drove them out with a whip.

A funny thing about this is that God was thought to be dwelling in the center of the temple. God's presence resided in the Holy of Holies in the center of the temple. Everything was good when God was where God was supposed to be. God could be managed. God could be boxed in. God could be controlled. God could be ignored. God could be turned into a profit-making machine.

But Jesus had been saying all along that the presence of God was no longer in the temple, but rather it was in him. Jesus was now the carrier of God's presence in the world, the full creative and redemptive power of creator God resided in Jesus, and Jesus was now dwelling with humanity in the outer court.

So when Jesus was turning over the tables in the temple, it was dangerous. Because God was not where God was supposed to be.

God's presence in the world was let loose through the incarnation of Jesus, and when it is let loose, it will turn over tables and fight injustice and bring restoration and renewal and establish new creation. God's presence makes everything new, and the powers that be don't want anything new. They like the way things are, they seek to maintain the status quo. God's presence is a dangerous presence!

God's presence was now residing in Jesus, but Jesus was very clear that he must leave so the Spirit could come. And this is what happened. After the resurrection and ascension of our Lord, the same presence that dwelt in Jesus now dwells in us. You and me.

As Jesus was ascending, he said to the disciples, "But you will receive power when the Holy Spirit comes on you; and you will be my witnesses in Jerusalem, and in all Judea and Samaria, and to the ends of the earth" (Acts 1:8).

This word for power is *dunamis*. This specifically is life-giving power. Power that is not meant for the owner, but is meant to be used as a conduit through the owner in order to bring shalom to the world. The power of the creative energy of the creation resides within you and is flowing through you. The dynamic power that raised Jesus from the grave resides within you and is meant to flow through you. The presence of God is now dwelling in you. As a follower of Jesus, the Holy Spirit—God's presence—is alive in you. Your job is to pour it out every chance you get.

Your life holds the potential to be a dangerous presence, but the only way you will be a danger to the powers of evil, injustice, segregation, fear, division, isolation, debt, and poverty is to allow that power to flow through you. How do you do this? I firmly believe that all you have to do is to go find suffering. Go find injustice. Go find oppression. Search it out. And then get close to it. So close you can touch it. Reside there. Make a dwelling there. Set up your home there. Set the table. You get close and the life-giving power of the resurrected Jesus will flow through you.

THE CITY

Jesus entered the city to face the systems of oppression. Will you? The people living in our cities are living under severe oppression and injustice. People created in the image of God are living under the oppression of poverty, racism, failed educational systems, unemployment, drugs, murder, prison, broken families, failed dreams, trauma, trafficking, rape, and hate. There are no other places where oppression is as intense as our cities. Yes, oppression and injustice exist in the suburbs and the countryside, but not like they do in our cities.

Our cities need you. They need the presence of God that lives within you. They need that presence that is a danger to the powers of evil to move through you to turn over tables of injustice and despair. They need you to stop living for yourself. They need you to stop living in fear. They need you to stop living behind your walls of division. They need you to stop trying to achieve the success of the American dream and live for God's dream! They need you.

And you need them. So many of us are isolating ourselves from the pain and injustice. We make excuses and start handing out blame, but all we are doing is destroying ourselves. Poverty is not "their fault." It's yours. It's ours. It's time we all take a little more responsibility for our neighbors. It's time we are moved to our bowels with *splangchonomazai*.

Henri Nouwen said, "Compassion . . . is not a bending toward the underprivileged from a privileged position; it is not a reaching out from on high to those who are less fortunate below; it is not a gesture of sympathy or pity for those who fail to make it in the upward pull. On the contrary, compassion means going directly to those people and places where suffering is most acute and building a home there."[3]

Our cities are so desperately hurting, and they need us. But not just our money, not just our charity or our pity or our presents. They need our presence, our lives. They need us to make intentional decisions to relocate and to live with and among them and say, "I'm here with you! I'm not leaving, and I will suffer with you and celebrate with you."

Don't live for yourself. Don't live for the American dream. That's a small life, a nightmare life. Live for the kingdom of God. Don't just take the job that pays the most money. Move into the city and live, serving God and those neighbors around you. Get involved in some hurting kids' lives in our cities. Become a mentor or tutor. You have skills and talents that God has given you. Live poured out. Redistribute those gifts, talents, skills, money. Give them away, and you will find life for yourself.

But remember, don't do this on your own. Find a local church who values these ideas we have discussed, and sit under them, be accountable to them, surround yourself with them. You will need a supporting community around you to hold you up and to hold you accountable. Don't do this on your own. Engage with the Christian Community Development Association (CCDA). Go to their conferences, read their books, absorb as much as you can from this amazing organization. They will teach you so much about relocation and reconciliation. They will say the hard things to you that no one else will.[4]

Sell your house and move into the city. Live in a hurting neighborhood. After you graduate college, get a job and live in the city and see the neighborhood as your home and your calling, the neighbors you are called to love and pour your life out for.

Worship Jesus, not money, power, success, fear, division, or isolation. Worship Jesus and serve your neighbors. Live in the image of God, not in the image of success.

Pastors and churches, there are hurting people all around you. Begin to pray that God would help you hear the cry of the oppressed in the cities near you. Be like Nehemiah. Fast and pray and mourn for the state of broken lives around you. Begin to teach your people about these things. Begin to disciple them in this way of worship. Partner with organizations that are bringing hope, healing, and restoration to our cities in a healthy and holistic way. Get people talking about urban ministry, relocation, and reconciliation. Form a team and commission them to begin a community assessment of your city. What are the real issues that are oppressing and dividing the people? Send people to a CCDA conference. Pastors and church leaders, it starts with you. If you go there, the people will go with you . . . maybe. I admit, it is a risky proposition. Yes, you will lose people. Yes, you may even lose your job. But we cannot ignore our cities any longer! They are crying out, and God is calling us to enter into this pain and suffering in order to bring hope and healing.

We have the dangerous presence living in us that fights evil and injustice. This is our calling, church, to live lives in surrender to Jesus, to live lives poured out, to live lives for something bigger than ourselves or *our* dreams. We are to live for God's dreams.

This is a risky life. It is dangerous to follow the one who is a dangerous presence. But if following Jesus is not costing you anything, then you are probably not really following Jesus. You are probably just watching as he passes you by. Maybe you have been shouting, "Hosanna!" But are you willing to shout, "Let my people go!"?

You are filled with this dangerous presence and called to be a dangerous presence to the powers that hold people down. Stand up and hear Jesus' call to you today as he looks deeply into your eyes and says, "Come, follow me. Follow me into the most hurting and desperate places."

You may indeed lose more than you were willing to give, but you will also find more than you expected to receive.

BENEDICTION

Now, may you follow Jesus into those hard places as he turns over the tables of injustice and division. May you hear the cry of the oppressed and be moved to your core. May you overcome the fear, division, and thirst for success that your culture has placed upon you and follow Jesus into the city. May you become a dangerous presence.

NOTES

CHAPTER 1

1. Google it; it's true. The United Nations estimates that it would take thirty billion dollars per year to end global hunger. Maybe we should start a campaign, "Give up ice cream—feed the world." Then we spend another forty-two billion dollars on diet-related products and services. Ironic, don't you think?

2. We also want our kids to drink more water and less sugar. Sugar is bad for you. I mean, really bad for you. Eat as little as possible!

3. For more depth on this and other Jewish-related ideas, read David H. Stern, *Jewish New Testament Commentary* (Clarksville, Md.: Jewish New Testament Publications, 1992).

4. A word to my Jewish friends here. Hold on. Jesus isn't done yet. He will establish his kingdom forever on this earth. Hope you haven't given up on him yet.

5. To learn more about the corrupt system of the temple in Jesus' day, read Richard Horsley, *Jesus and the Powers: Conflict, Covenant, and the Hope of the Poor* (Minneapolis: Fortress, 2011). Describing this, Horsley says, "When Herod's son Archelaus proved unsatisfactory as a client ruler, the Romans resorted again to the priestly aristocracy to control Judea and Samaria and to collect the tribute. Now, however, they placed the high priesthood under the supervision, and military backup, of a Roman governor based in Caesarea. Since the governors usually exercised the power of appointment, it was incumbent on the four high priestly families from which the high priest might be appointed to maintain close collaboration with the governors. These high priestly families became increasingly wealthy during the first century. They maintained private gangs of strongmen, apparently for their own security as well as to implement their predatory appropriation of the people's crops" (p. 36).

6. See Ched Myers, *Binding the Strong Man: A Political Reading of Mark's Story of Jesus* (Maryknoll, N.Y.: Orbis, 1988, 2008). Myers says of the temple, "Thus Jesus calls for an end to the entire cultic system—symbolized by his

'overturning' . . . of the stations used by these two groups. They represented the concrete mechanisms of oppression within a political economy that doubly exploited the poor and unclean. Not only were they considered second-class citizens, but the cult [temple] obligated them to make reparation, through sacrifices, for their inferior status—from which the marketers profited" (p. 301).

7. "Human-diminishing activity" is a term I borrowed from N. T. Wright.

CHAPTER 2

1. I attended Asbury Theological Seminary in Wilmore, Kentucky. I'd like to give a shout out to Dr. Darrell Whiteman, who first introduced me to the idea of incarnational missions. Thanks, Dr. Whiteman! Live with the people. Listen to the people. Love the people. Brilliant.

2. A person once asked me, "Is there such a thing as non-rural Appalachia?" Yes, there is, actually. Blacksburg, Asheville, and Roanoke are some non-rural Appalachian towns.

3. This is one of the nicknames given to Milwaukee because of all the brewing factories here, the most prominent being Miller Brewing.

4. For more on the "cry" and how it inaugurates history, read Walter Brueggemann, *Prophetic Imagination*, 2nd ed. (Minneapolis: Augsburg Fortress, 2001), or any other book by him.

5. Richard Rohr, *Everything Belongs: The Gift of Contemplative Prayer*, rev. ed. (New York: Crossroad, 2003).

6. Les Christie, CNN Money, last updated April 5, 2012, http://money.cnn.com/galleries/2012/real_estate/1204/gallery.US-Cities/ index.html.

7. *The American Heritage Dictionary of the English Language*, 4th ed., s.v. "paternalism."

8. A great book to look at this further is Robert Lupton, *Toxic Charity: How Churches and Charities Hurt Those They Help (And How to Reverse It)* (New York: Harper, 2012).

CHAPTER 3

1. Please don't take my analogy here to the extreme to say that I think we should let our kids do ridiculously crazy and absolutely dangerous things. Parents need to provide boundaries, of course, and protect our children, but we also need to let them experience things for themselves.

2. "LeBron James Extends Charity Efforts," ESPN NBA, last updated March 2, 2011, http://sports.espn.go.com/nba/truehoop/miamiheat/news/story?id=6175574.

3. Miroslav Volf, *A Public Faith: How Followers of Christ Should Serve the Common Good* (Grand Rapids, Mich.: Brazos, 2011), 57.

4. Ibid., 61.

CHAPTER 4

1. The mission statement of our church—Transformation City Church—is, "To live out the way of Jesus within a multiracial community that seeks to bring hope, healing, restoration, and salvation to all people."

2. You can read more about this ministry at www.inhabitmke.org.

CHAPTER 5

1. *Riding Giants*, directed by Stacy Peralta (2004; Topanga, Calif.: Agi Orsi Productions). You can find clips of this on YouTube.

2. Ibid.

3. Ibid.

4. Abraham Joshua Heschel, *The Prophets* (New York: HarperCollins, 2001), 4.

5. Walter Brueggemann, *The Prophetic Imagination*, rev. ed. (Minneapolis: Augsburg Fortress, 2001), 39.

6. Ibid., 37.

7. Ibid., 14.

8. Gabe Lyons, *The Next Christians: Seven Ways You Can Live the Gospel and Restore the World* (Colorado Springs: Multnomah, 2012).

9. For more information, visit http://qideas.org.

CHAPTER 6

1. Larry Sandler, "Milwaukee Property Values See Biggest Drop in 30 Years," *Journal Sentinel*, April 27, 2012, http://www.jsonline.com/news/milwaukee/milwaukee-property-values-see-biggest-drop-in-30-years-v556or2-149315155.html.

2. Read more about Common Ground at www.commongroundwi.org.

3. Martin Luther King, Jr., *Strength to Love* (Minneapolis: Fortress, 2010), 59.

4. Read more about International Justice Mission at www.ijm.org.

5. Jesse Garza, "Prostitution Crackdown Targets Human Trafficking," *Journal Sentinel*, June 25, 2012, http://www.jsonline.com/news/crime/53-prostitutes-3-pimps-rounded-up-in-milwaukee-west-allis-and-oak-creek-q85t9nm-160318 465.html.

6. Read more about Exploit No More at www.esploitnomore.org.

7. Gabe Lyons, *The Next Christians: Seven Ways You Can Live the Gospel and Restore the World* (Colorado Springs: Multnomah, 2012), 25.

CHAPTER 7

1. Richard Rohr, *Everything Belongs: The Gift of Contemplative Prayer* (New York: Crossroad, 2003) is a great reminder of the need to let go of competition and realize we have all we need.

2. Tom Daykin, "Sale of Paradise Theater Building to Church Completed, Repairs to Begin," *Journal Sentinel*, June 15, 2011, http://www.jsonline.com/business/123969914.html.

3. Tom Daykin, "Greenfield Walmart Being Sold to Church," *Journal Sentinel*, June 15, 2012, http://www.jsonline.com/blogs/business/ 159091085.html.

4. Ben Parman, "All for One," Transformation City Church (blog), October 3, 2011, http://transformationcity.blogspot.com/search?q=all+for+one.

5. Bruce Malina and Richard Rohrbaugh, *Social-Science Commentary on the Synoptic Gospels*, 2nd ed. (Minneapolis: Augsburg Fortress, 2003), 336.

6. Ched Myers and Elaine Enns, *Ambassadors of Reconciliation: New Testament Reflections on Restorative Justice and Peacemaking*, vol. 1 (Maryknoll, N.Y.: Orbis, 2009), 58.

7. In 2011 Milwaukee was ranked as the most segregated city in the US. Daniel Denvir, "The 10 Most Segregated Urban Areas in America," Salon, March 29, 2011, http://www.salon.com/2011/03/29/most_segregated_cities/slide_show/10.

CHAPTER 8

1. Check them out online at www.theedgechurch.com. Read about Pastor Troy's powerful story too: Troy A. Evans, *The Edge of Redemption: A Story of Hope for Rescuing the Unreachable* (Indianapolis: Wesleyan Publishing House, 2011).

2. The Daniel fast is a fast that basically abstains from meats, breads, sugars, and dairy products. In our culture today, perhaps we need to recapture this diet, subverting the empire of food in our country, foods that are killing us and giving us heart attacks and diabetes. Maybe the church needs to recapture this message. Every year I give a sermon on food and some people are angered by it. I encourage people to stop eating sugar, limit breads, eat more vegetables, and when they eat meat, eat sustainable, grass-fed meat and dairy. And stop drinking soda. I encourage you to talk to your doctor about the Daniel fast and to research it on your own.

3. Walter Wink, *The Powers That Be: Theology for a New Millennium* (New York: Doubleday, 1998), 82.

4. For more on living in this nightmare, read Anthony de Mello, *Awareness: The Perils and Opportunities of Reality* (New York: Doubleday, 1990).

5. C. S. Lewis, *God in the Dock* (n.p., 1970), 58.

CHAPTER 9

1. Nicholas Wolterstorff, "The Grace That Shaped My Life," in *Finding God at Harvard: Spiritual Journeys of Thinking Christians*, ed. Kelly Monroe Kullberg, rev. ed. (Downers Grove, Ill.: InterVarsity Press, 2007), 156.

2. Nicholas Wolterstorff, *Justice in Love* (Grand Rapids, Mich.: Eerdmans, 2011). Wolterstorff uses to describe *agape* love in action: self-sacrificing love that seeks to benefit the other, seeks the human flourishing of our neighbors.

3. See David H. Stern, *Jewish New Testament Commentary* (Clarksville, Md.: Jewish New Testament Publications, 1992).

4. Wolterstorff, *Justice in Love*, 109.

5. Let's be careful not to hold capitalism up too high. The great missiologist Lesslie Newbigin says this of capitalism in light of the fall of socialism in Russia: "The ideology of the free market now has nothing to limit its claims. There is no visible countervailing power. There seems no sign of a check to its relentless advance. And its destructive potential, both for the coherence of human society and for the safeguarding of the environment, are formidable. The ideology of the free market has proved itself more powerful than Marxism. It is, of course, not just a way of arranging economic affairs. It has deep roots in the human soul. It can be met and mastered only at a level of religious faith, for it is a form of idolatry. The churches have hardly begun to recognize that this is probably their most urgent missionary task during the coming century" (*The Open Secret* [Grand Rapids, Mich.: Eerdmans, 1995], 94–95).

6. Ibid., 97.

CHAPTER 10

1. Novella Ruffin, "Children and Stress: Caring Strategies to Guide Children," Virginia Cooperative Extension, Virginia State University (May 1, 2009): 350–054, http://pubs.ext.vt.edu/ 350/350-054/350-054.html.

2. You can read more about the political climate of first-century Israel in Richard Horsley, *Jesus and the Powers: Conflict, Covenant, and the Hope of the Poor* (Minneapolis: Fortress, 2011).

3. A brilliant book to read about the connection between our cities and prison is Michelle Alexander, *The New Jim Crow: Mass Incarceration in the Age of Colorblindness* (New York: New Press, 2012).

4. Vincent Felitti et al., "Relationship of Childhood Abuse and Household Dysfunction to Many of the Leading Causes of Death in Adults: The Adverse Childhood Experiences (ACE) Study," *American Journal of Preventative Medicine* 14, no. 4 (May 1998): 245–258, accessed August 7, 2013, http://www.ajpmonline.org/article/S0749-3797(98)00017-8/fulltext.

5. "Trauma-Informed Care and Trauma Services," Substance Abuse and Mental Health Services Administration, accessed August 7, 2013, www.samhsa.gov/nctic/trauma.asp.

6. Howard Bath, "The Three Pillars of Trauma-Informed Care," *Reclaiming Journal* 17, no. 3 (Fall 2002).

7. Joachim Jeremias, *The Eucharistic Words of Jesus* (Norwich, UK: SCM Press, 2011), n.p.

CHAPTER 11

1. *The Usual Suspects*, directed by Bryan Singer (Beverly Hills, Calif.: Metro-Goldwyn-Mayer Studios, 1995).

2. Michael Frost, *Exiles: Living Missionally in a Post-Christian Culture* (Peabody, Mass.: Hendrickson, 2006), 13. Frost is referring here to the rabbits in the novel *Watership Down* by Richard Adams. That's why rabbits are part of the quote.

3. Ibid., 15.

4. Chris Rice and Emmanuel Katongole, "A Christian Vision for Reconciliation," *Divinity*, Spring 2012, http://divinity. duke.edu/community-student-life/diversity-magazine/spring-2012/christian-vision-reconciliation/page/0/1.

CHAPTER 12

1. For more about Revelation, read Gordon Fee, *Revelation*, New Covenant Commentary Series (Eugene, Ore.: Cascade, 2011); or Michael Gorman, *Reading Revelation Responsibly: Uncivil Worship and Witness—Following the Lamb into the New Creation* (Eugene, Ore.: Cascade, 2011).

2. For more about how controversial this would have been to the Roman powers, read Richard Horsley, *Jesus and the Powers: Conflict, Covenant, and the Hope of the Poor* (Minneapolis: Fortress, 2011); specifically pages 155–178.

3. Donald P. McNeill, Douglas A. Morrison, and Henri Nouwen, *Compassion: A Reflection on the Christian Life*, rev. ed. (New York: Doubleday, 1982), 23.

4. For more information, check out the CCDA website: www.ccda.org.